DESIRE

Erotic Poetry Through
the Ages

Edited by William Packard

Foreword by Richard Eberhart

ST. MARTIN'S PRESS
New York

Manufactured in the United States of America

Library of Congress Cataloging in Publication Data

Main entry under title:

Desire, erotic poetry through the ages.

1. Erotic poetry.   I. Packard, William.
PN6110.E65D4   808.81'93538   80-14234
ISBN 0-312-19469-2

DESIGN BY DENNIS J. GRASTORF

10 9 8 7 6 5 4 3 2 1
First Edition

Table of Contents

Acknowledgments

The editor wishes to thank the authors, their publishers, and their representatives for their kind permission to reprint poems and translations and prose excerpts in this anthology of erotic poetry, as follows:

In the editor's introduction, translations by Frederick Goldin from *Lyrics of the Troubadours and Trouveres*. Introduction, notes and translations by Frederick Goldin; copyright © 1973 by Frederick Goldin. Reprinted by permission of Doubleday & Co., Inc.

"Alone," "To Eros," "The Blast of Love," "Seizure," "Paralysis," "From Aphrodite," "The Death of Adonis," "Sleep," "Song for the Bride," "Shall I?", "One Night," "Remorse," "To a Handsome Man," "Ungiven Love," "When You Come," "I Would Fly," "Her Friends," and "Eros," from *Greek Lyric Poetry*, translated by Willis Barnstone. Copyright © 1962–1967 by Bantam Books; reprinted by permission of Willis Barnstone and Bantam Books, all rights reserved.

Chapters 2, 4, and 5, from *The Song of Solomon*, the King James Version of The Holy Bible.

"That the Mere Glimpse," "Plop Fall the Plums," "I Beg of You," "That Mad Boy," "By the Clearing," and "High Spurt the Waters," from *The Book of Songs*, translated by Arthur Waley, copyright © 1960 by Grove Press, reprinted by permission of Grove Press, Inc.

"For a Moment," translated by William Packard, copyright © 1970 by William Packard, reprinted by permission of William Packard.

"Sparrow," "Dress Now," "Come, Lesbia," "Flavius," "Poor Damned Catullus," "O Mellow," "He Is Changed," "You Are the Cause," "Lesbia Speaks," "I Hate and Love," and "Lesbia, Forever Spitting Fire," translated with an introduction by Horace Gregory, from *The Poems of Catullus*, copyright © 1956 by Horace Gregory, published in The Norton Library Edition, 1972. W. W. Norton & Co., Inc. Reprinted by permission of Horace Gregory.

"I Am No Ordinary Coward," "Lonely and Silent," "What's to Do First?", "How We Rejoiced," "She's Torn From Me," "Whoever First Portrayed Love," "Not Even Agamemnon," "If You Must Lie to Me," and "All My Filled Notebooks Lost," translated from the poems of Sextus Propertius by Constance Carrier, copyright © 1963 by The Indiana University Press, reprinted by permission of Constance Carrier and The Indiana University Press.

"Apollo and Daphne," "Jove and Europa," "Echo and Narcissus," "Mars and Venus," "Pygmalion," "Venus and Adonis," "Orpheus and Eurydice," translated by Horace Gregory from Ovid's *Metamorphoses*, copyright © 1958 by The Viking Press, Inc., reprinted by permission of Horace Gregory and The Viking Press.

Excerpts from *The Satyricon* of Petronius, translated by William Arrowsmith, copyright © 1959 by William Arrowsmith, reprinted by arrangement with The New American Libraries, Inc.

"Restless and Discontent," "I Have Two Sicknesses," "I Know I Am Poor," "Didyme Waved Her Wand," "Get Drunk My Boy," "Lysidike Dedicates," "What Are You Saving It For?", "Your Flatteries Are Boring," "You Are the Most Beautiful," "I Swear by Desire," "Nothing Is Sweeter Than Love," "I Have Sworn Ten Thousand Times," "Eros Has Changed His Quiver," "You're Right, Lais' Smile," "Fornication Is a Filthy Business," "Good God, What a Night That Was," "I Had Just Gone to Bed," "That Night Will Long Delight Us," "Waking, My Eyes," "Hello. Hello," and "In the Middle of the Night," translated by Kenneth Rexroth from *The Greek Anthology*, copyright © 1962 by The University of Michigan Press, reprinted by permission of Kenneth Rexroth and The University of Michigan Press, Ann Arbor.

"The Advantages of Learning," from *The Collected Shorter Poems of Kenneth Rexroth*, copyright © 1944 by New Directions. Reprinted by permission of Kenneth Rexroth and New Directions Publishing Corporation.

"Doing, a Filthy Pleasure Is," translated by Ben Jonson from *The Greek Anthology*.

La Vita Nuova by Dante Alighieri, translated by Dante Gabriel Rosetti, from *The Viking Portable Dante*, copyright © 1947 by The Viking Press, reprinted by permission of The Viking Press.

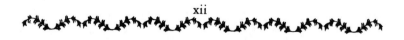

Foreword

When asked to write a foreword to an anthology of erotic poetry, my first impulse was to say no. I had preconceived notions about the value of such an enterprise. Why should anybody read a body of erotic poetry when the subject is minor compared with the whole of poetry? Must we be titillated by poetry? Must we descend to erotic delight in poetry? When you think of the massive greatness of the art and that it deals with the harsh realities of man's fate in his short duration on earth, with struggle, effort, ambition, with hope, and with despair and with eventual, inevitable death, why should readers not read, or read again, the great exemplars of the art, Dante, Shakespeare, Milton, Wordsworth, Keats, and the masters of our own century; why waste time on anything an erotic poem could say?

There is a long-lasting body of erotic poetry, in the East and in the West, and it has given, and can and does give its special type of delight. It is no less human than the most lofty sentiments expressed by Chinese, Indian, Moslem, or English-speaking poets past or present. There is something to be said for erotic poetry that the more erotic it is the better. Here we come into a trap of love. There have been many great love poems in all languages, and indeed love is one of the central and fundamental topics of poetry, but where will the critic find the fine dividing line between love poetry and erotic poetry? There is much love poetry that is not erotic; there is erotic poetry that is sensual but not about love. We slide into semantic difficulties and quarrels here.

Webster gives erotic as "of, devoted to, or tending to arouse sexual love or desire." Love is described as "the attraction, desire, or affection felt for a person who arouses delight or admiration or elicits tenderness, sympathetic interest, or benevolence." One of the most moving passages of love poetry is the Francesca passage in Canto V of *The Inferno*. It reads (in Ciardi's translation):

> On a day for alliance we read the rhyme
> of Lancelot, how love had mastered him.
> We were alone with innocence and dim time.
>
> Pause after pause that high old story drew
> our eyes together while we blushed and paled;
> but it was one soft passage overthrew
>
> our caution and our hearts. For when we read
> how her fond smile was kissed by such a lover,
> he who is one with me alive and dead

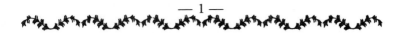

breathed on my lips the tremor of his kiss.
That book, and he who wrote it, was a pander.
That day we read no further.

"That book" was certainly an erotic book and in this passage it is fair to say that love and eroticism are joined together.

If the intellect gets a hold on us too hard it may make us say what is the use of erotic poetry, why should we read erotic poetry instead of going directly to the flesh? Is erotic poetry any good compared to the real thing? It must be considered good, because there are so many good erotic poems by great poets through the centuries and in all languages, but I go back to my original statement that it is not in my view the richest resource of poetry, is percentage-wise probably only a small fraction of poetry, and not as meaningful as the major examples about life, death, suffering, joy, time and fate, but is a special kind of poetry calling for special responses, which are freely given. Compare, for instance, the Canto V quotation with the weight of the whole *Inferno*.

This book gives the reader a wide spectrum of pleasures in this special genre.

Jack Vaughn, then head of the Peace Corps, sent me to Kenya in 1966 to interview our volunteers. While there I was taken by Land Rover to see the wild animals. They could not endanger you if you stayed in the vehicle. Having stopped by some lions lying in the sun our driver saw afar what he said he had not seen for eight years, lions copulating. Would we like to stalk them? We would. He drove over. I had my movie camera ready and we saw lion and lioness in the act of copulation. It was a great sight, especially when afterward they walked majestically across the plain. I learned that lions copulate only once a year but for about seventy-four hours every half an hour. Nature is thus bound to make the female pregnant, she is drenched with future life, and thus the race is preserved and life continues. Think of the seriousness of purpose of this event. The seriousness of it! Yet man is the only animal who copulates any time of the day or night at all times of the year, and can make love into a game of pleasure as well as a function of regeneration. Man has developed the erotic as a spice of life. And for centuries men and women have written erotic poems along with all other kinds of poems.

Here is the poem I wrote about the vivid African experience:

LIONS COPULATING

We caught lions copulating on the plains
Of Africa. Our landrover closed in.
I pressed so hard on my 8mm. color film
I almost lost this gigantic naturalism,

Trying to preserve it for my friends and astoundees.
But saw the King of Beasts with his head high,
His mane imperial, no expression on his face,
Prodding in and out of the great female

As if he were a schizophrenic dualist
And had to put up with his baser nature,
For his great face had no expression at all
While his lower being worked mechanical,

Then he fell away, and stood off, and lay
His full length on the ancient earth
While the lioness with a sumptuous gesture
Rolled over as I have seen other females do

In the perfect surfeit of her animal nature,
And took ease as if nobody were looking on,
And after an interval of valuable rest
These great beasts of the African wilds

Stood in their historic posture of superiority
And ambled across the limitless plains in silence
Without of thought of the lucubration of man,
Trying to signify their big natures in empathy.

> NAIROBI (*from* Collected Poems
> 1930-1976, 1976 *Oxford
> University Press, New
> York, and Chatto &
> Windus, London.*)

I don't suppose that this is an erotic poem, according to the Webster definition given above, but I wanted to present it as tangential. To conclude, erotic poetry, an ancient but minor part of world poetry, is made up of the good, the funny, the laughable or amusing, and the vile, the base or cheap. This book provides all categories. There is something for everybody. William Packard has supplied the reader with an able history of erotic poetry through the centuries.

The book is richer in its earlier representations than in its later ones. Splendid examples are given from Sappho, the Old Testament, Chinese, Greek, and Roman works. Western poems from the Medieval time through the Renaissance are plentiful, and coming later in the book are comic limericks, as well as explicit sexual poems. Mr. Packard has a commendably broad view of the dimensions of his subject. Who would

think that Dowson's "Vitae Summa Brevis" would be found here, or Emerson's "Give All to Love," or Ben Jonson's "To Celia," Herrick's "To the Virgins, to Make Much of Time," or Waller's "Go, Lovely Rose," indeed a host of famous love poems scarcely erotic? Such entries enrich the volume against the erosion of some too grossly explicit poems. All told, and all known, the book gives good coverage to an ancient, uncovered subject.

RICHARD EBERHART

Introduction

What is Desire?

We all know what Desire feels like—it is something that comes on us unexpectedly from somewhere out there in the air, and when it hits us it is an insect itch, a slow corrosion of our lower areas; it is a trouble in the bloodstream and the pulse of possibility in all our body parts.

That's what it feels like all right, but what is the root of Desire, what is Eros itself? After all, we build up almost all our social systems around some vague idea of what Eros really is—all our family structures, our morals, our mores, our laws, even our religions. And our popular American behavioral psychologists tell us what we should do about all our so-called "sex problems"—as if Eros itself were some sort of a given, some sort of a constant natural force like electricity that is a trustworthy thing, and if it is not working properly in our lives then it must be because of our own hangups. And all these sexologists seem to be saying that if we could only get in touch with ourselves, then Eros would flow through us and everything would work itself out okay.

But whether Eros is really all that constant or trustworthy is not so clear. Because all the oracles and all the stories of Greek mythology would seem to be saying otherwise. And if you were to go outside right now onto the street to take a random sampling of people to see what they thought Eros was all about, you'd probably come back with some pretty wildly divergent ideas, such as the following:

Eros is whatever turns you on.

Eros is anything that is dirty and filthy and you shouldn't allow people to read books about it or see it on TV or go to movies where it is shown in explicit detail.

Eros is something that sends out invisible wave lengths that go right through you like laser beams and it is also all that spooky full moon madness of A Midsummer Night's Dream that creates these huge lunatic delusions and it makes you do the most foolish things imaginable.

Eros is something you only really feel with only one person that you truly love and so you must never dream of ever experiencing Eros with anyone other than this one person that you truly love.

And after listening to so many wildly divergent ideas about Eros, you may find yourself saying that the whole thing is relative, and that one man's Eros is another man's impotence. But then when you yourself sit down and try to define your own idea of Eros, and when you come on all these curious longings and hungers inside yourself for something you feel you lack, then you may finally decide that Eros is one of the most elusive

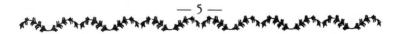

things in the whole universe. Because all you really know for sure is that Eros is in the air right there where you are, and that it is all around you always, so much so that sometimes you may even wish that it would go away.

Perhaps we can begin to get a sense of what Eros is all about if we see what some of our most outstanding minds have had to say about it. To begin with, Eros may be much more than just our own personal sexual feelings—it may be a part of some larger rhythmic energy that pervades the entire universe. George Santayana suggests this in *The Idea of Christ in the Gospels:*

Eros in the Greek poets and philosophers represented natura naturans, *the potentiality in matter working as in a seed and unfolding itself in every form of life. It is only by poetic license that the unfolding of* natura naturans *can be called love. That process is something unconscious, unpremeditated, unalloyed, always going on best in profound slumber. . . .*

Santayana seems to be hinting here that Eros may be some mysterious primal force that initiates all the alchemy and all the transformations in nature—that is, it may be a magical energy field, a physical flux like the Hindu procreative power Sacti that pervades all of nature.

Then again, Eros may be something quite unaccountable, something so deeply paradoxical and irrational that our consciousness cannot contain it as a simple idea. Carl Jung describes sexuality itself as "chthonic," that is, of God and the devil simultaneously.

Then again, Eros may have very little to do with the object that gives rise to the feelings of eroticism. Sigmund Freud writes:

The most profound difference between the love life of antiquity and our own lies in the fact that the ancients placed the emphasis on the instinct itself whereas we put it on the object. The ancients extolled the instinct and were ready to ennoble through it even an inferior object, while we disparage the activity of the instinct as such and only countenance it on account of the merits of the object.

> —footnote, *The Sexual Aberrations*
> from *Three Contributions to the*
> *Theory of Sex*

That is, the Greeks could get off on their own horniness, and celebrate it as such, without associating it with whatever triggered that horniness in the first place.

These modern interpretations are all very well, but if we are ever to get back to an understanding of what the Greeks themselves really thought Eros was all about, we would have to go to the myth of who Eros was and what he was up to. Here is the story of Eros:

Eros was a beautiful winged youth, the mischievous imp child of Aphrodite who was the goddess of Love. Eros used to go with Aphrodite on all her amorous adventures, and Eros would be armed with a bow and arrows so he could shoot his arrows of desire at both gods and men and cause them to fall in love. In gang language, Eros was Aphrodite's hit man—Eros would make the initial sexual contact, then Aphrodite would move in to do the really serious business of love.

Once there was a young girl named Psyche (soul) who was so beautiful that Aphrodite grew furious with jealousy and she swore she would make Psyche sorry for being so beautiful. Aphrodite told Eros to wound Psyche with an arrow and so Eros flew to where Psyche was sleeping, but Psyche woke up and she saw Eros, and Eros was so startled at being seen that he wounded himself with one of his own arrows of desire, and that was when he fell in love with Psyche. The two of them were married but Eros told Psyche that she was never to look at him, that he would only come to make love to her in the dark of night, but one night Psyche lit a lamp so she could look at Eros and Eros flew away in fear and distrust. But the lovers were soon reunited and Psyche was made immortal so the two could love each other forever, and they had a daughter whose name was Pleasure.

What are we to make of all this? Eros is an imp child, mischievous and curiously mercurial, as quick to fly in as to fly out, and like a child, Eros has no inhibitions at all—he will shoot his arrows of desire at the unlikeliest times and in the unlikeliest places, and whoever gets hit by one of these arrows of Eros will experience a paradoxical longing and hunger that may never go away. In the second part of the story, the human soul is told not to look at its own eroticism, but the soul looks anyway—that is, spirituality and sexuality are posited as polar opposites, although they are still inextricably linked together inside of us.

Yet if Eros is so central in all our lives, why is he depicted as a child god? Why not a chief god? The answer is that the Greeks in their wisdom could never bring themselves to make a chief god out of such an irrational and mischievous deity as Eros. Robert Graves writes in *The Greek Myths:* "Eros was never considered a sufficiently responsible god to figure among the ruling Olympians of Twelve."

Still, the Greeks did worship Eros, and incessantly. They set up pillars with giant upright stone phalloses, and these Priapus stones were everywhere—Priapus was the son of Dionysos, and was represented by a large upright cock. And this Priapus statue was in gardens, to scare starlings away; it was on Greek vases, where naked satyrs ran around in acrobatic copulation with nymphs, or gangbangs, or mutual masturbations; and it survives down to our own day as a twisted horseshoe (bent Priapus) hanging over a doorway, and as our annual May Pole. It has been estimated that there have

been more disciples of Priapus than of any other religious figure in the history of the world.

The only thing about Eros and eroticism that the Greeks did not openly worship was the repression of Eros. Sexuality was always out there in the open sunlight for everyone to see, and this openness is reflected in the poetry of the Greeks. In Book 8 of the *Odyssey,* Homer tells the story of how Hephaistos traps his wife Aphrodite in a great net with her lover Ares, and then Hephaistos calls for all the other gods to come and see:

> *Come see this pair entwining here*
> *in my own bed! How hot it makes me burn!*
>
> *I think they may not care to lie much longer,*
> *pressing on one another, passionate lovers;*
> *they'll have enough of bed together soon . . .*

The Greek gods respond as only the Greek gods could respond to such a sight:

> *. . . and irrepressible among them all*
> *arose the laughter of the happy gods.*
>
> *(tr. Robert Fitzgerald)*

Apollo turns to Hermes and he asks: "Would you let yourself get all chained up like that, if you could lie next to the naked Aphrodite?" Hermes answers: "You could wrap me in three times as many chains, just so I could lie next to the naked whiteness of the goddess Aphrodite!"

This may seem odd to us, for a husband to call all the gods to laugh at the spectacle of his own wife caught in the act with her lover. But then the Greeks had a remarkably different attitude towards Eros than we have.

Probably the greatest poet of Eros was the Greek lyric poet Sappho, who lived sometime in the middle of the 7th century B.C. on the island of Lesbos in Mytelene. We know Sappho was married, that she had a daughter named Cleis, and that she gathered together a group of women around her to teach music and poetry and to share in the worship of Aphrodite. Sappho wrote some nine books of odes and elegies and hymns, although only a few fragments have come down to us—even so, these brief verses are among the most incandescent poetry ever written.

Greek tragedy itself began with the celebration of Dionysos, god of fertility, and the tragedies were punctuated by satyr plays where goat-footed Pan figures raced across the stage with grotesque erect phalloses. And although the tragedies dealt with man's relation to the gods and to himself, the plays were never very far from Eros. Perhaps the most famous example of the Greeks' attitude towards Eros is the comedy by

persuades the women of Athens and Sparta and Boetia to swear off having sex with their husbands for the duration of the Peloponnesian Wars, until the men come to their senses and agree to lay down their arms and live in peace. In the following scene, Cinesias comes onstage with a large erection and he tries to get his wife Myrrhine to come to bed with him:

Cinesias: Let's make love right now, Myrrhine!

Myrrhine: What, in front of the baby?

Cinesias: The slave will take it home. Now lie down!

Myrrhine: But where?

Cinesias: Over there, by the park of Pan.

Myrrhine: But how could I cleanse myself afterwards?

Cinesias: Easy, just wash in the spring.

Myrrhine: But what about the vow I took?

Cinesias: I'll answer for that.

Myrrhine: Well all right, only let me get a bed.

Cinesias: We won't need a bed, the ground will do.

Myrrhine: No no, bad as you are, you can't lie on the ground. (EXITS)

Cinesias: I think she must really love me.

Myrrhine: (ENTERS) Here's the bed, lie down and I'll take my clothes off. No wait, we need a mattress.

Cinesias: We don't need a mattress.

Myrrhine: Yes we do, it's no good on bare springs.

Cinesias: Come kiss me.

Myrrhine: I'll be right back. (EXITS)

Cinesias: My god, hurry!

Myrrhine: (ENTERS) Here's the mattress, lie down and I'll take all my clothes off—no wait, we don't have a pillow!

Cinesias: We don't need a pillow.

Myrrhine: Of course we do! (EXITS)

Cinesias: My god, what's all this teasing?

Myrrhine: (ENTERS) Here, lift your head. Now is that all?

Cinesias: That's all, now come over here.

Myrrhine: I'm taking all my clothes off, but remember your promise.

Cinesias: I swear to all the gods.

Myrrhine: We don't have a blanket.

Cinesias: We don't need a blanket!

Myrrhine: I'll be right back. (EXITS)

Cinesias: I'm fed up with all this bedding!

Myrrhine: (ENTERS) Here, get up for a moment.

Cinesias: I've got *this* up!

Myrrhine: Do you want some perfume?

Cinesias: Ye gods, no.

Myrrhine: Yes, we'll need some perfume. (EXITS)

Cinesias: Curses on perfumes!

Myrrhine: (ENTERS) Here, give me your hand.

Cinesias: All I smell is delay.

Myrrhine: Then this must be the wrong perfume.

Cinesias: Never mind!

Myrrhine: Don't be silly! (EXITS)

Cinesias: To hell with whoever invented perfume!

Myrrhine: (ENTERS) Here, this is a bigger thing.

Cinesias: I've got an even bigger thing right here! Lie down.

Myrrhine: Wait 'til I take my shoes off. Remember, you promised to vote for peace.

Cinesias: I'll think about it. (MYRRHINE EXITS) Oh Zeus, what tortures I go through!

(tr. Packard)

What a modern audience would find laughable—the sight of a man with a large erection who is being teased out of his mind by an evasive woman—the Greek audience would find both laughable and serious at the same time, because the Greeks knew that such a condition could occasion very great pain and distress.

The same Aristophanes who wrote *Lysistrata* was also present at the famous banquet that Plato (427–347 B.C.) writes about in the *Symposium,* which presents almost all the classical ideas about love. In this dialogue, Socrates gives his own definition of Eros:

Socrates: . . . Then he and every one who desires, desires
    that which he has not already, and which is future
    and not present, and which he has not, and is not,
    and of which he is in want . . .

(tr. Jowett)

Eros then is a seeking after that which we do not yet have—it is a longing or a hunger for something we lack. And other civilizations have treated Eros or Desire in pretty much the same way. It is a consuming hunger or longing in the Peking Opera *The White Snake* by Tyan Han, where there is this drunken Boatman's song:

> These are good days on West Lake,
> as we go through wind and rain—
> ten lifetimes to meet a mate,
> then a hundred to embrace.

(tr. Packard)

The literal translation of the last two lines is something like this:

it takes ten lifetimes to meet the right mate
and it takes ten times ten lifetimes for these two heads to lie
    down together next to each other on the same pillow.

The song is an outcry against the odds of our ever finding what we are looking for in our deepest desires.

In Japanese art there are drawings of lovers that are extremely explicit, showing every conceivable position of love, as in the erotic Indian temple reliefs, or the *Kama Sutra,* where the art of love becomes a manual on the mechanics of Eros:

    The Deer-Woman, whose Yoni is six fingers deep;
    The Mare-Woman, whose Yoni is nine fingers deep;
    The Elephant-Woman, whose Yoni is twelve fingers deep;
    . . .
    The Hare-Man, whose Lingam is six finger breadths;
    The Bull-Man, whose Lingam is nine finger breadths;
    The Horse-Man, whose Lingam is twelve finger breadths . . .

In the Holy Bible, Eros is incorporated into the Genesis Creation myth, as Eve is created out of the bone of Adam's rib and then she is tempted by the phallic serpent. There is phallic worship throughout the Old Testament (e.g. Genesis 35:14; 11 Samuel 6:20), and the Song of Solomon is one of the most erotic of all allegorical love poems, with an aching of the soul for the beloved:

Stay me with flagons, comfort me with apples: for I am sick of
    love.

In Roman literature a curious thing happens to Eros—he is translated into "Cupid" and thereby loses a great deal of his dark power and divinity. "Cupid" is cute, whereas Eros is in deadly earnest, relentless and intense. And perhaps because eroticism has been stripped of its transcendental origins, the Roman life style strikes us as more pagan and power-oriented than in touch with the various warring divinities within the human soul. The Roman excesses are monstrous: it was rumored that Nero had relations with his own mother, Agrippina; that he married a man, Doryphones; and that he caused the death of one of his wives, Poppaea Sabina, by kicking her in the stomach while she was pregnant. And the so-called sports that took place inside the later Roman Colosseum had

nothing, nothing whatever to do with Eros—they were the very lowest form of voyeurism and bloodthirstiness.

Of all the Roman poets, Gaius Valerius Catullus 84–54 B.C. comes closest to an awareness of Eros. Catullus went to Rome in 62 B.C. where he met a woman he calls "Lesbia" (she was probably Clodia, wife of Metellus Celer who was Proconsul of Cisalpine Gaul). Catullus wrote poem after poem for Lesbia, pouring his genius into the immediate passion and misery of Eros—and as he wrote the brightest celebrations of delight, he also wrote the most sullen outbursts of loathing. We have every reason to believe that Catullus was right in his accusations of all the things Lesbia did, not the least of which was that she was unfaithful to Catullus with at least "three hundred others."

Of the other Roman poets, Sextus Propertius lived in Rome 60–16 B.C., knew Ovid and Horace, and wrote poems for "Cynthia" (probably Hosita, a courtesan). His poems were melancholy, sincere and self-pitying as he wasted away in his desires. And Publius Ovidius Naso, Ovid (43 B.C.–A.D. 18), wrote *The Art of Love (Ars Amatoria)*, in which he argued that all women could be had if only one could learn the proper approach to them. This book was probably the cause of Ovid's banishment from Rome in A.D. 8 by Augustus, although the book is a charming account of the various vagaries and strategems of the game of love, as in these lines translated by Guy Lee, published by Viking Press, 1968:

xib

Love and hate, here in my heart, at tug of war—
and love I suppose will find a way to win.

I'd sooner hate. If I can't I'll be the reluctant lover—
the dumb ox bearing the yoke he loathes.

Your behavior drives me away, your beauty draws me back.
I adore your face and abhor your failings.

With or without you life's impossible
and I can't decide what I want.

Why can't you be less lovely or more true?
Why must your faults and your figure clash?

I love what you are and hate what you do—
but your self, alas, outweighs your selfishness.

By the bed we shared, by all the gods
who let you take their names in vain,

By your face my holy icon, by your eyes that ravished mine,
take pity on me.

Be what you will you'll still be mine—but you must choose—

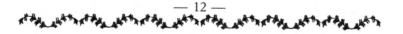

do you want me to want to love you or be forced to?

Make life plain sailing for me please
by helping me love what I can't help loving.

In the *Metamorphoses,* Ovid tells story after story from the Greek myths, illustrating all the curious alchemies and transformations of love and sexuality. Gaius Petronius Arbiter (d. A.D. 65) wrote the *Satyricon,* a ribald, picaresque novel about his adventures in southern Italy and centering on a banquet of Trimalchio. And in the *Greek Anthology* (compiled sometime around A.D. 917), Petronius argues for the right to write about the eroticism of his own life:

> Why do you frown on me, you puritans?
> And condemn the honesty of my latest poems?
> Be thankful for fine writing
> That makes you laugh instead of weep.
> What people do, an honest tongue can talk about.
> Do you know anybody who doesn't enjoy
> Feasting and venery?
> Who forbad my member to grow hot in a warm bed?
>
> Father Epicurus himself commanded us
> To become really sophisticated in this art.
> Furthermore, he said this was the life of the gods.
>
> *(tr. Kenneth Rexroth)*

Roman art depicts a kind of pagan Eros—coins show couples fornicating, and the frescoes at Pompeii show men and women in gymnastic intercourse, the women usually on top; young girls are about to go down on the cocks of bearded older men; and a man stands holding a pair of scales in his hand, so that he can weigh his erect male member in its full tumescence. There are no gods here, only human beings describing their own behavior.

With the decline of the Roman empire, the idea of Eros experienced a further translation that is still a source of very real confusion in the modern world. As the medieval world began to construct its colossal architecture of repression, it saw that Eros was nothing but a mischievous imp child, and there was no place for him in the Gothic cathedral of order and strict limitation on the human mind and heart. And so Eros was officially designated as "lust," one of the seven deadly sins, and as such it was seen as an extension of the sin of pride. In the *City of God,* Book XIV, Augustine says that Original Sin was occasioned by Lust, and he goes on to imagine an ideal form of procreation where the genitals perform their functions by an act of will:

. . . to beget children without this lust, so that in this function of begetting offspring the members created for this purpose should not be stimulated by the heat of lust, but should be actuated by his volition, in the same way as his other members serve him for their respective ends.

It is difficult to imagine trying to sustain such a volitional hard-on, but that is exactly what Augustine has in mind.

Later, Thomas Aquinas in the *Summa Theologica* (Q 84, Article 4) describes lust as a distortion, a dysfunction, an inordinate desire for sexual intercourse, something that is a defect of moral character. Thus Eros becomes, for the medieval world, not an autonomous power outside the individual as it was for the Greeks, but a personality defect that is within the individual himself. The idea of Eros is thus consigned to the realm of pagan myth, and it becomes a dead thing.

Yet the underlying saga of sexuality keeps right on going, in the guise of courtly love. Eros makes its way into medieval romance in the Anglo-Saxon scops, the chanters; in Wales, the Bards; elsewhere, the minstrels, the oral troubadours, the trouveres, the storytellers, the jongleurs, and the 12th century fabliau in the medieval romance languages—Provençal, Italian, French, Spanish and Portuguese. These stories all glorify chivalry and show boredom with feudal marriages and the subordinate role of women. The greatest of these stories is *Tristan and Ysolt,* written in 1210, and is an example of *minne* or romantic love—the lovers drink a love potion unwittingly and its magic power makes them forget their own wills, so thereafter they love each other above all things. In medieval French, the verse is poignant:

> Isolt ma drue, Isolt m'amie,
> En vous ma mort, en vous ma vie!

Guillaume IX (1071-1127) was a troubadour poet who announced his mission of Eros in the following astounding line:

> dirai vox de con, cals es sa leis

> (I will tell you of cunt, and of its laws)

Frederick Goldin writes in his introduction to *Lyrics of the Troubadours and Trouveres:*

Under the rule of the *leis de con* all actions have the status of accidents, for this "law" allows no motive but instinctual appetite in the individual, and no other rule but chance in the world. Everyone wanders around till he or she bumps into

someone else, and then lust astounds them both with its possibilities . . . .

This "law of the cunt" turns the whole world into a singles bar, in which nothing is real except the next sexual escapade. Only Eros remains, and the will to go on in an endless longing and hunger for love, as in the poetry of Arnaut Daniel 1150–1200:

> I am in her service
> from my foot to my hair . . . .
>
> *(tr. Frederick Goldin)*

There is also bitterness and an endless wandering through the world, as in the poetry of Bertran de Born (born around 1140):

> Lady, since you do not care for me
> and have sent me away
> without any cause,
> I do not know whether to give my love,
> for never
> will I find such noble joy
> again . . . .
>
> *(tr. Frederick Goldin)*

Courtly love finds its highest expression in the poetry of Dante Alighieri (1265–1321). In 1274, on May Day, Dante was nine and Beatrice Portinari was eight when Dante glimpsed Beatrice for the first time, and thereafter he dedicated his life to recording his love for her. This was an apotheosis of Eros; even though Dante and Beatrice never touched each other and they each went on to marry other persons, Dante places Beatrice in the very highest regions of his Paradiso. But elsewhere in the *Commedia*, Dante punishes all those souls who ever gave way to Eros in their own lives—he places the "carnal sinners" like Cleopatra, Helen, Paris, Tristram, Dido, Francesca da Rimini, Lancelot and Guinevere, in the lower regions of the Inferno where they are blown about forever on the stormy restless winds of their own passions. And in the Paradiso, Dante defines heaven as the absence of Eros, when Picardia says:

Brother, the quality of love stilleth our will,
   and maketh us long only for what we have
   and giveth us no other thirst . . .

Francesco Petrarca (Petrarch) 1304–1374, first glimpsed his Laura in 1327, and devoted the next thirty-one years of his life to writing sonnets in praise of his love for her.

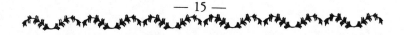

In early English poetry, Eros makes itself felt in verses such as *Westron Winde,* which the American poet Richard Eberhart calls "one of the great love poems of all time":

> Westron winde, when wilt thou blow,
> The smalle raine down can raine?
> Crist, if my love wer in my armis,
> And I in my bed againe.

We also feel the presence of Eros in the great early English ballads, such as *Ladie Greensleeves:*

> Alas, my love, ye do me wrong,
>   To cast me off discurteously:
> And I have loved you so long,
>   Delighting in your companie.

With Geoffrey Chaucer (1340–1400), we feel Eros in the air, a fertile presence in the Prologue to the *Canterbury Tales,* where April actually makes a sexual penetration of March and pours its liquid life into the new spring:

> Whan that Aprille with his shoures sote
> The droghte of Marche hath perced to the rote,
> And bathed every veyne in swich licour
> Of which vertu engendered is the flour . . .

And in his ballad of *Merciles Beaute: A Triple Rondel,* Chaucer describes how the arrows of Eros enter into the eyes and render someone completely helpless:

> Your yen two wol slee me sodenly,
> I may the beaute of hem not sustene,
> So woundeth hit through-out my herte kene . . . .

Nowhere is the enthrallment and desolation of Eros felt more keenly than in Chaucer's *Troilus and Criseide*—after Troilus first sees Criseide and is stricken into a swoon and lies in bed long days, he sings the *Cantus Troili:*

> If no love is, O god, what fele I so?
> And if love is, what thing and whiche is he?
> If love be good, from whennes cometh my wo?
> If it be wikke, a wonder thinketh me,
> When every torment and adversiteee
> That cometh of him, may to me savory thinke;
> For ay thurst I, the more that I it drinke.

As the humanists began to write more and more in their own vernacular language, their poetry began to run the full range of Eros—Rabelais (1494–1553); Boccaccio (1313–1375) in the *Decameron;* and Pietro Aretino in *Putana Errante,* "The Wandering Whore." One example of early English Eros folk poetry is the *Second Shepherds Play* (circa 1425–1450), written in Middle English by the Wakefield Master for the Towneley Cycle of pageant plays. The play is filled with a naive fascination for all the natural body functions, erotic and scatological, and there is also a scathing attack on medieval marriages:

> I'm telling you, these married men lead a bad life,
> Even the newlyweds have a lot of strife,
> the husband is led around by the wife
> and in bed it gets as sharp as a knife,
>> night after night.
> I know it now,
> if you make a vow,
> you may allow
>> someone to get you tied uptight.

(tr. Packard)

The Renaissance was a resurgence of the human spirit in painting and poetry and sculpture and philosophy, with an honest return to Eros and a worship of the human body for its own sake. One way to feel this Renaissance of Eros is to think of two images: the *Birth of Venus* by Sandro Botticelli (1445–1510), where a naked woman rises from the sea; she is curious, sad, languid, sensuous and awakening, as if the mother of Eros had been caught in a rare instant of air. The second image is the Mona Lisa by Leonardo da Vinci (1452–1519), with that mysterious smile which may be the smile of Eros itself: it is serene, elusive, ethereal, seductive, voluptuous, animal, mischievous, but also subtly mocking, sinister, and perhaps even fatal. It is interesting to compare this smile of Eros with the gloomy view Leonardo took of the human genitals in his own notebooks:

The act of procreation and the members employed therein are so repulsive, that if it were not for the beauty of the faces and the adornment of the actors and the pent-up impulse, nature would lose the human species.

The Renaissance of Eros can be felt in the poetry of Michelangelo Buonarrotti (1465–1564), who met Vittoria Colonna about 1542 and later wrote passionate sonnets to her. And there is Renaissance Eros in the marvelous verse of Christopher Marlowe (1564–1593), who believed Eros struck at a single blow, as in these lines from *Hero and Leander:*

> Where both deliberate, the love is slight,
> Who ever lov'd, that lov'd not at first sight?

The sonnets of Shakespeare (1564–1616) are rare outpourings of Eros, and the last two sonnets in the sequence of 154 poems are about Eros himself, the "little child god." Surely the entire balcony scene in *Romeo and Juliet* is one of the most exalted celebrations of Eros ever written, and for the sheer pathos of the errors of Eros there is the mad song of Ophelia in *Hamlet:*

> By gis, and by Saint Charity,
>   Alack and fie for shame:
> Young men will do't, if they come to't,
>   By cock they are to blame.
> Quoth she: Before you tumbled me,
>   You promised me to wed:
> So would I ha' done by yonder Sun,
>   And thou hadst not come to my bed . . .

John Donne (1571–1631) wrote some of the greatest erotic poems in our language, and Donne had the gift of fusing his strong sexual passion with a very real religious energy, as in *The Good Morrow, The Sunne Rising, The Relique* and the mock cynical *Go and Catch a Falling Star.*

In France, we have the neoclassic theatre of Racine (1639–1699), and in *Phèdre,* Hippolyte tries to repress his erotic love for Aricie until it suddenly bursts forth in a torrential force. And later in France, the Marquis de Sade was, according to one author, "The cruellest debauchee, the lewdest writer, and the most persistent propagator of immorality the world ever saw."

But at this point in time a curious thing began to happen—Eros was beginning to grate on later ages, and the forces of repression began to set in. Alexander Pope published an expurgated edition of Shakespeare in 1725, and in 1818 Thomas Bowdler published an abridged edition in which entire passages of Shakespeare were either excised or altered beyond recognition. Obscenity began to be prosecuted in the courts; the Victorian era saw the rise of the middle classes and with them, a repression of Eros that was so furious that sometimes even the legs of grand pianos had to be covered over. But simultaneous with this repression there grew up a tremendous underground—Hogarth made his erotic engravings, John Cleland wrote his famous *Fanny Hill,* and there were innumerable books and pamphlets that began to explore such so-called forbidden areas as fetishism, bestiality, flagellation, necrophilia, circumcision, aphrodisiacs, deflowering of virgins, hermaphrodites, transsexualism, to say nothing of incest, rape, and seduction of the very young. There were such odd and curious and witty little books as: *The Adventures of a School-boy; or, The Freaks of Youthful Passion* (1866); *The Adventures of Miss Lais Lovecock, at Miss Twig's Boarding School* (1792); *The Adventures of Sir Henry Loveall*

(1860); *The Amorous Friars; or, The Intrigues of a Convent* (1759); *The Widow and the Parson's Bull* (1792); and *The Gentleman's Spicey Reciter*. And there was quaint doggerel, such as these lines from *The Amorous Quaker:*

> Shove her down on the bed, or up against the wall,
> Shove her backwards, forwards, or any way at all . . .

"The Dying Lover to His Prick" was an 18-line poem that mocked Shelley's *Indian Serenade* and Saint Paul, both at the same time:

> Lend, lend your hand! I mount! I die!
> O Prick, how great thy Victory?
> O Pleasure, sweet thy stings.

This poem caused a stir for its blasphemous allusions, but it was nothing compared to the uproar made by the "Essay on Woman" that was a parody of Alexander Pope's "Essay on Man"—Horace Walpole called this "the most blasphemous and indecent poem that ever was composed." It contains these lines:

> Hope humbly then clean Girls; nor vainly soar;
> But fuck the Cunt at hand, and God adore.
> What future Fucks he gives not thee to know,
> But gives that Cunt to be thy Blessing now.

In 1763, *The Gentleman's Magazine* attacked this "Essay on Woman," and John Wilkes was tried and convicted of publishing the poem. The poem was called to the attention of the House of Lords by Lord Sandwich, although this only created a demand for more copies. This was soon followed by *Lady Bumtickler's Revels* published in 1777, the same year as Sheridan's *School for Scandal*. And for sheer lunacy one couldn't come up with a flakier title than *Cythera's Hymnal; or, Flackes from the Foreskin. A Collection of Songs, Poems, Nursery Rhymes, Quiddities, Etc., Etc. Never Before Published. Oxford: Printed at the University Press, For the Society for Promoting Useful Knowledge.* 1830. One poem contained in this book has this verse:

> The shades of night were falling fast,
> As up and down the High-street passed
> A youth, who bore inside his gown
> A prick-stand he could not keep down—
> Chordee! Chordee!

Another book, *The Blowen's Cabinet*, contains such song titles as: *Oh, Miss Tabitha Ticklecock!!!* and *The Magical Carrot; or, The Parsley Bed* and

Going a Nesting! and *The Lost Cow!!! or, The Bulling Matche under the Tree.*
Lord Byron was rumored to have authored *Don Leon,* a poem of 1455 lines
in praise of anal intercourse, which he practiced with his wife when she
was great with child; the poem contains these lines:

> All comers by the usual door refuse,
> And let the favored few the back stairs use.

Robert Burns (1759–1796) had a bawdy "flair for fatherhood,"
tumbling his bonnie lasses in the fields and then writing heartfelt lyrics on
the risks of Eros and the occasional anguish of heartache after:

> How can ye chant, ye little birds,
> And I sae fu' o' care?

John Keats (1795–1821) in his short lifetime may have felt more of the
enthrallment and desolation of Eros than any poet of modern time, yet
hardly any of this Eros was ever acted out beyond the printed page. In his
short poem *La Belle Dame Sans Merci,* Keats shows us the terrible
aftermath of Eros and its devastation on the human spirit.

Walt Whitman (1819–1892) included in *Leaves of Grass* an account of
the generative energies called "Children of Adam." Ralph Waldo Emerson
tried to talk Whitman out of publishing it, and Whitman listened
respectfully as Emerson argued, but then Whitman went right ahead and
published it anyway. Whitman lost his job as clerk in the Indian Bureau
of the Department of the Interior, when Interior Secretary Harlan found
out Whitman was the author of "an indecent book."

Probably the most notorious form of Eros in modern poetry is the
limerick—often foolish, sometimes loony five-liners that can claim their
ancestry as verse form all the way back to Shakespeare's *King Lear.* These
modern, anonymous dactyls are filled with surprise anglo-saxonisms, and
they trace their first appearance back to 1846, after Edward Lear had
published his *Book of Nonsense,* and the English magazine *Punch* took up
Lear's limerick form and offered a place-name limerick contest—"There
was a young lady from Cheshire," etc. . . . and the fun was on. Even
Swinburne contributed a few limericks to world literature.

Meanwhile modern poets were beginning to return to the seriousness of
Eros as a real power. The German poet Rainer Maria Rilke wrote a sonnet
"Eros" in 1924 that is terrifying in its description of the ways we try to
keep from facing the naked stare of Eros:

> Faces! Faces! We keep making faces.
> Else how could we bear his naked stare?
> Bright sunlight shines in hidden places
> Shaming all our playful foreplay there.

One is talking and for no real reason
Suddenly becomes dumb . . . Something wails . . .
Shudderings run through like a season . . .
He dresses her in great sacred veils.

And now she is lost, is lost forever!
Gods take us in such desperate leaps.
She is reborn somehow, however.
Somewhere far inside a sad voice weeps.

(tr. Anne Katcher, English version
by William Packard)

Frederico Garcia Lorca believed Eros was *duende,* a dark power outside ourselves that was " . . . a power and not a behavior, it is a struggle and not a concept . . . of blood; of ancient culture; of creative action. . . ." Lorca wrote two of the most erotic lines ever written in his poem *The Unfaithful Wife:*

Her thighs escape me
like two silver fish . . .

(tr. Packard)

The French poet Paul Verlaine, in *Femmes/Hombres,* wrote bi-sexual poems based on his experiences with Arthur Rimbaud. Other modern poets, such as Yeats, H.D., and Pierre Louÿs (in his prose poems) paid serious tribute to the role of Eros in all our lives.

But along with the modern world's attempt to return once more to Eros in earnest, the forces of repression began to try to ostracize and outlaw any and all expressions of eroticism. Henry Miller's early novels, *The Tropic of Cancer* and *The Tropic of Capricorn,* were written in Europe and for generations they were contraband items, only reaching this country hidden away in the suitcases of American tourists returning home from abroad. In 1927, Bennett Cerf defended the publication of James Joyce's *Ulysses,* in a landmark decision that allowed the classic to be printed and distributed in the United States. Kenneth Patchen was denied advertising space in *The New York Times* for his novel *Memoirs of a Shy Pornographer,* not because the book was pornographic (it isn't), but because the title evoked a subject matter the editors feared might offend the readership. And the first editions of Allen Ginsberg's *Howl* were printed with asterisks in place of key words ("with mother finally ******"). The book was seized by the U.S. Customs when it was shipped into this country from the printer abroad, and there was an obscenity trial in San Francisco—at which literary figures testified as to the serious intention of the poem— before *Howl* was allowed to circulate freely in this country.

If we think seriously about this exercise of free speech, we realize we cannot make sense out of it unless we make a few vital distinctions. Pornography is any transaction in obscenity for the sake of money (*obscena* means quite literally "that which cannot be shown on stage"), whereas eroticism is a complex element that combines almost all the primal forces of poetry and civilization. One way of separating eroticism from obscenity is to ask: how much is at stake? In pornography, all that is at stake is the price of admission, or the fee that is paid to the actors, or the models, or the authors who turn out the stuff. The sexuality is held off at arm's length so we can leer at it and be sated. With eroticism, however, a great deal is always at stake. The author or the artist or the actor has allowed us to enter into an experience of his or her own sexuality, and to share in the crucial risk of Eros, to experience the torment and joy of arousal and realization. As such, eroticism can be an indispensable insight into the human condition. What D.H. Lawrence was really against in his essay "Pornography and Obscenity" was the sneakiness of sex, "the dirty little secret." He was all for "the creative portrayal of the sexual impulse that we have in Boccaccio or the Greek vase paintings or some Pompeiian art, and which are necessary for the fulfillment of our consciousness." Lawrence felt pornography was merely the attempt to "insult sex, to do dirt on it. This is unpardonable."

The contemporary poems in this book include the work of such poets as Richard Eberhart, Kenneth Patchen, Anne Sexton, Theodore Roethke, Leonard Cohen, G. G. Belli, Dylan Thomas, Hart Crane, Irving Layton, John Betjeman, Richard Howard, J. V. Cunningham, Erica Jong, Judson Jerome, Siv Cedering, Michael Harlow, and May Sarton. I am proud that some of the poems in this anthology were originally published in *The New York Quarterly*, which I edit—poems by Muriel Rukeyser, Charles Bukowski, Linda King, John Updike, Jean Balderston, Jackson MacLow, Lola Haskins, Vivian Shipley-Jokl, Lisa Ritchie, Patricia Farewell, and Leo Connellan. There are a number of prose works I would have liked to include in an anthology of this kind: excerpts from *The Tale of Genji* by Lady Murasaki, A.D. 1001; *The Decameron* of Boccaccio; *Justine* by the Marquis de Sade; *My Life and Loves* by Frank Harris; *Our Lady of the Flowers* by Jean Genet; *Delta Autumn* by Anaïs Nin; and the novels of Henry Miller. I am glad to be using prose excerpts from Kenneth Patchen's *The Journal of Albion Moonlight*, Vladimir Nabokov's *Lolita*, and Jerzy Kosinski's *Passion Play*.

In compiling this anthology, I have used a very broad reading of the word Eros, as I have tried to explain in this introduction, and I hope the general reader will find the book interesting and useful without further footnotes. I hope also that the book will find its way into our classrooms, as we have a great deal to learn about the ways of Eros in our world.

The literature of Eros is vast, and a very great deal of it is still underground. I'm inclined to think that much of this underground stuff is vastly overrated, and I'm also. inclined to think that generally we are not living in a particularly erotic age, although we like to think that we are. Erratic behavior is no substitute for a worship of Eros, who is a dark god of tremendous power and original energy, and he will have his way with us if we do not set our hearts and minds in opposition to him.

By way of Bibliography I would recommend all of the classical authors that are mentioned in this introduction, and I would also like to list here, in no particular order, some of the other books I have found of special interest:

THE ENCYCLOPEDIA OF EROTIC LITERATURE (3 volumes);
Pisanus Fraxi; Documentary Books, Inc.; 1962.
(Original publication: 1877).

EROTIC POETRY; edited by William Cole;
Random House; 1963.

A HISTORY OF EROTICISM; Ove Brusendorll and
Poul Henningsen; Lyle Stuart, Inc. 1963.

POETICA EROTICA; T. R. Smith; Crown; 1921.

LYRICS OF THE TROUBADOURS AND TROUVERES;
edited by Frederick Goldin; Anchor; 1973.

From Sappho

ALONE

The moon and Pleiades
are set. Night is half
gone and time speeds by.
I lie in bed, alone.

TO EROS

You burn me.

THE BLAST OF LOVE

Like a mountain whirlwind
punishing the oak trees
love shattered my heart.

SEIZURE

To me that man equals a god
as he sits before you and listens
closely to your sweet voice

and lovely daughter—which troubles
the heart in my ribs. For now
as I look at you my voice fails,

my tongue is broken and thin fire
runs like a thief through my body.
My eyes are dead to light, my ears

pound, and sweat pours down over me.
I shudder, I am paler than grass,
and am intimate with dying—but

I must suffer everything, being poor.

PARALYSIS

Mother darling, I cannot work the loom
for sweet Kypris has almost crushed me,
broken me with love for a slender boy.

FROM APHRODITE

I tell you, Sappho,
love is my servant.

THE DEATH OF ADONIS

Our tender Adonis is dying, O Kythereia,
What can we do?
Beat on your breasts, my girls, and tear
your dresses.

SLEEP

May you find sleep on a
soft girlfriend's breast.

SONG FOR THE BRIDE

No girl who ever was,
O groom, was like her.

SHALL I?

I do not know what to do:
I say yes—and then no.

ONE NIGHT

All the while, believe me, I prayed
our night would last twice as long.

REMORSE

Do I still long
for my virginity?

TO A HANDSOME MAN

Stand up and gaze on me as friend
to friend. I ask you to reveal
the naked beauty of your eyes.

UNGIVEN LOVE

I am dirty with longing
and I hunger for her.

WHEN YOU COME

You will lie down and
I shall lay out soft
pillows for your body.

I WOULD FLY TO THE VERY FOOT
OF YOUR MOUNTAINS

I would go anywhere
to take you in my arms
again, my darling.

HER FRIENDS

No, my heart can never change
toward you who are so lovely.

EROS

Now in my
heart I
see clearly

a beautiful
face
shining,

etched
by love.

(tr. Willis Barnstone)

From The Song of Solomon
Chapter 2

I am the rose of Sharon, and the
lily of the valleys.
2 As the lily among thorns, so is
my love among the daughters.
3 As the apple tree among the
trees of the wood, so is my beloved
among the sons. I sat down under
his shadow with great delight, and
his fruit was sweet to my taste.
4 He brought me to the banqueting
house, and his banner over me
was love.
5 Stay me with flagons, comfort
me with apples: for I am sick of
love.
6 His left hand is under my head,
and his right hand doth embrace
me.
7 I charge you, O ye daughters of
Jerusalem, by the roes, and by the
hinds of the field, that ye stir not up,
nor awake my love, till he please.
8 The voice of my beloved!
behold, he cometh leaping upon
the mountains, skipping upon the
hills.
9 My beloved is like a roe or a
young hart: behold, he standeth
behind our wall, he looketh forth
at the windows, shewing himself
through the lattice.
10 My beloved spake, and said
unto me, Rise up, my love, my fair
one, and come away.
11 For, lo, the winter is past, the
rain is over and gone;
12 The flowers appear on the
earth; the time of the singing of
birds is come, and the voice of the

turtle is heard in our land;
13 The fig tree putteth forth her
green figs, and the vines with the
tender grape give a good smell.
Arise, my love, my fair one, and
come away.
14 O my dove, that art in the
clefts of the rock, in the secret places
of the stairs, let me see thy counte-
nance, let me hear thy voice; for
sweet is thy voice, and thy counte-
nance is comely.
15 Take us the foxes, the little
foxes, that spoil the vines: for our
vines have tender grapes.
16 My beloved is mine, and I am
his: he feedeth among the lilies.
17 Until the day break, and the
shadows flee away, turn, my beloved,
and be thou like a roe or a young
hart upon the mountains of
Bether.

Chapter 4

Behold, thou art fair, my love;
behold, thou art fair; thou hast
doves' eyes within thy locks: thy
hair is as a flock of goats, that ap-
pear from mount Gilead.
2 Thy teeth are like a flock of sheep
that are even shorn, which came up
from the washing; whereof every
one can bear twins, and none is barren
among them.
3 Thy lips are like a thread of scar-
let, and thy speech is comely: thy
temples are like a piece of a pome-
granate within thy locks.
4 Thy neck is like the tower of
David builded for an armoury,
whereon there hang a thousand
bucklers, all shields of mighty men.
5 Thy two breasts are like two
young roes that are twins, which
feed among the lilies.

6 Until the day break, and the
shadows flee away, I will get me to
the mountain of myrrh, and to the
hill of frankincense.
7 Thou art all fair, my love; there
is no spot in thee.
8 Come with me from Lebanon,
my spouse, with me from Lebanon:
look from the top of Amana, from
the top of Shenir and Hermon,
from the lions' dens, from the
mountains of the leopards.
9 Thou hast ravished my heart, my
sister, my spouse; thou hast ravished
my heart with one of thine eyes,
with one chain of thy neck.
10 How fair is thy love, my sister,
my spouse! how much better is thy
love than wine! and the smell of
thine ointments than all spices!
11 Thy lips, O my spouse, drop as
the honeycomb: honey and milk
are under thy tongue; and the smell
of thy garments is like the smell of
Lebanon.
12 A garden enclosed is my sister,
my spouse; a spring shut up, a foun-
tain sealed.
13 Thy plants are an orchard of
pomegranates, with pleasant fruits;
camphire, with spikenard,
14 Spikenard and saffron; cala-
mus and cinnamon, with all trees of
frankincense; myrrh and aloes, with
all the chief spices:
15 A fountain of gardens, a well
of living waters, and streams from
Lebanon.
16 Awake, O north wind; and
come, thou south; blow upon my
garden, that the spices thereof may
flow out. Let my beloved come
into his garden, and eat his pleasant
fruits.

Chapter 5

I am come into my garden, my
sister, my spouse: I have gathered
my myrrh with my spice; I have
eaten my honeycomb with my hon-
ey; I have drunk my wine with my
milk: eat, O friends; drink, yea,
drink abundantly, O beloved.

2 I sleep, but my heart waketh:
it is the voice of my beloved that
knocketh, saying, Open to me, my
sister, my love, my dove, my unde-
filed: for my head is filled with dew,
and my locks with the drops of the night.

3 I have put off my coat; how shall
I put it on? I have washed my feet;
how shall I defile them?

4 My beloved put in his hand by
the hole of the door, and my bowels
were moved for him.

5 I arose up to open to my beloved;
and my hands dropped with myrrh,
and my fingers with sweet
smelling myrrh, upon the handles of
the lock.

6 I opened to my beloved; but my
beloved had withdrawn himself, and
was gone: my soul failed when he
spake: I sought him, but I could not
find him; I called him, but he gave
me no answer.

7 The watchmen that went about
the city found me, they smote me,
they wounded me; the keepers of
the walls took away my veil from
me.

8 I charge you, O daughters of
Jerusalem, if ye find my beloved,
that ye tell him, that I am sick of
love.

9 What is thy beloved more

than another beloved, O thou fairest
among women? what is thy beloved
more than another beloved, that
thou dost so charge us?
10 My beloved is white and ruddy,
the chiefest among ten thousand.
11 His head is as the most fine
gold, his locks are bushy, and black
as a raven.
12 His eyes are as the eyes of doves
by the rivers of waters, washed with
milk, and fitly set.
13 His cheeks are as a bed of
spices, as sweet flowers: his lips like
lilies, dropping sweet smelling
myrrh.
14 His hands are as gold rings set
with the beryl: his belly is as bright
ivory overlaid with sapphires.
15 His legs are as pillars of marble,
set upon sockets of fine gold:
his countenance is as Lebanon, ex-
cellent as the cedars.
16 His mouth is most sweet: yea,
he is altogether lovely. This is my
beloved, and this is my friend, O
daughters of Jerusalem.

(tr. King James Bible)

From The Book of Songs

10

That the mere glimpse of a plain cap
Could harry me with such longing,
Cause pain so dire!

That the mere glimpse of a plain coat
Could stab my heart with grief!
Enough! Take me with you to your home.

That a mere glimpse of plain leggings
Could tie my heart in tangles!
Enough! Let us two be one.

17

Plop fall the plums; but there are still seven.
Let those gentlemen that would court me
Come while it is lucky!

Plop fall the plums; there are still three.
Let any gentleman that would court me
Come before it is too late!

Plop fall the plums; in shallow baskets we lay them.
Any gentleman who would court me
Had better speak while there is time.

I beg of you, Chung Tzu,
Do not climb into our homestead,
Do not break the willows we have planted.
Not that I mind about the willows,
But I am afraid of my father and mother.
Chung Tzu I dearly love;
But of what my father and mother say
Indeed I am afriad.

I beg of you, Chung Tzu,
Do not climb over our wall,
Do not break the mulberry-trees we have
    planted.
Not that I mind about the mulberry-trees,
But I am afraid of my brothers.
Chung Tzu I dearly love;
But of what my brothers say
Indeed I am afraid.

I beg of you, Chung Tzu,
Do not climb into our garden,
Do not break the hard-wood we have planted.
Not that I mind about the hard-wood,
But I am afraid of what people will say.
Chung Tzu I dearly love;
But of all that people will say
Indeed I am afraid.

That mad boy
Will not speak with me
Yes, all because of you
I leave my rice untouched.

That mad boy
Will not eat with me.
Yes, it is all because of you
That I cannot take my rest.

48

He. By the clearing at the Eastern Gate
Where madder grows on the bank—
Strange that the house should be so near
Yet the person distant indeed!

She. By the chestnut-trees at the Eastern Gate
Where there is a row of houses.
It is not that I do not love you,
But that you are slow to court me.

High spurt the waters of that fountain,
Yet it flows back into the Ch'i.
My love is in Wei,
No day but I think of him.
Dear are my many cousins;
It would be well to take counsel with them:

'On the journey you will lodge at Tzŭ,
You will drink the cup of parting at Ni,
A girl that goes to be married,
Leaving parents, leaving brothers,'
I will ask all my aunts
And next, my elder sister:

'On the journey you will lodge at Kan;
You will drink the cup of parting at Yen,'
Grease wheels, look to axle-caps,
And the returning carriages will go their way:
"A quick journey to the Court of Wei,
And may you get there safe and sound."

I think of the Forked Fountain,
Long now I sigh for it.
I think of Mei and Ts'ao,
And how my heart yearns!
Come, yoke the horses, let us drive away,
That I may be rid at last of my pain.

(tr. Arthur Waley)

FOR A MOMENT

For a moment, unaware,
weary, I fell asleep.
My handsome young man,
who is determined to win,
riding his brown horse,
visited me. On the
low bed we lay down
and gently slept. This
may have been a dream.

May have been a dream.

WIN PE
*(tr. from the Burmese
by William
Packard)*

From Catullus

2

Sparrow, O, sweet sparrow,
love of my lady love,
she who's always nursing
you between her breasts and
feeding you her finger-tips;
she, that radiant lady,
delicious in her play with you,
for a while forgetting
all the deeper wounds of love . . .
I envy her. This pastime
would raise my heart from darkness.

Dress now in sorrow, O all
you shades of Venus,
and your little cupids weep.

My girl has lost her darling sparrow;
he is dead, her precious toy
that she loved more than her two eyes,
O, honeyed sparrow following her
as a girl follows her mother,
never to leave her breast, but tripping
now here, now there, and always singing
his sweet falsetto
song to her alone.

Now he is gone; poor creature,
lost in darkness,
to a sad place
from which no one returns.

O ravenous hell!
My evil hatred rises against your power,
you that devour
all things beautiful;
and now this pitiful, broken sparrow,
who is the cause of my girl's grief,
making her eyes weary and red with sorrow.

Come, Lesbia, let us live and love,
nor give a damn what sour old men say.
The sun that sets may rise again
but when our light has sunk into the earth, it is gone forever.
    Give me a thousand kisses,
then a hundred, another thousand,
another hundred
    and in one breath
still kiss another thousand,
another hundred.
    O then with lips and bodies joined
many deep thousands;
    confuse
their number,
    so that poor fools and cuckolds (envious
even now) shall never
learn our wealth and curse us
with their
evil eyes.

Flavius, if your girl friend
were not a little bastard,
you'd be telling your Catullus
all about her charms forever.
Now I know the story:
she's some feverish little bitch
that's warm and sweet and dirty
and you can't get up the nerve
to tell me that you love her.
Not a word! Look at your bed
still trembling with your labours
(tell me that you sleep alone)
sheets soiled with love and flowers,
and why, why?
   Look at your poor loins
all bruised and empty.
No matter who she is or why,
I'll immortalize you
and your dear young lady
in a blushing blissful song
that echoes against heaven.

8

Poor damned Catullus, here's no time for nonsense,
open your eyes, O idiot, innocent boy, look at what has
    happened:
once there were sunlit days when you followed after
where ever a girl would go, she loved with greater
love than any woman knew.
Then you took your pleasure
and the girl was not unwilling. Those were the bright days,
    gone;
now she's no longer yielding; you must be, poor idiot,
more like a man! not running after
her your mind all tears; stand firm, insensitive.
say with a smile, voice steady, "Good-bye, my girl,"
    Catullus
strong and manly no longer follows you, nor comes when
    you are calling
him at night and you shall need him.
You whore! Where's your man to cling to, who will praise
    your beauty,
where's the man that you love and who will call you his,
and when you fall to kissing, whose lips will you devour?
But always, your Catullus will be as firm as rock is.

O Mellow, sweet, delicious little
piece, my Ipsithilla,
I love you dearly.
Tell me to come at noon
and I'll come galloping
at your threshold.
Let no one bar the door today
but stay at home, my little one,
to fit yourself for nine long
bouts of love. And if you're so inclined,
call me at once;
my morning meal is over
and I reclining
discover
my tree of life (your bedfellow)
has risen joyfully tearing through my clothes,
impatient to be at you.

51

He is changed to a god he who looks on her,
godlike he shines when he's seated beside her,
immortal joy to gaze and hear the fall of
    her sweet laughter.

All of my senses are lost and confounded;
Lesbia rises before me and trembling
I sink into earth and swift dissolution
    seizes my body.

Limbs are pierced with fire and the heavy tongue fails,
ears resound with noise of distant storms forever
    into deep midnight.

* * * * * *

This languid madness destroys you Catullus,
long day and night shall be desolate, broken,
as long ago ancient kings and rich cities
    fell into ruin.

75

You are the cause of this destruction, Lesbia,
that has fallen upon my mind;
this mind that has ruined itself
by fatal constancy.
And now it cannot rise from its own misery
to wish that you become
best of women, nor can it fail
to love you even though all is lost and you destroy
all hope.

Lesbia speaks evil of me with her husband near and he
    (damned idiot) loves to hear her.
Chuckling, the fool is happy, seeing nothing, understanding
    nothing.
If she forgetting me fell silent, her heart would be his alone,
content and peaceful;
but she raves, spitting hatred upon me, all of which carries
this meaning:
I am never out of her mind, and what is more, she rises in
fury against me
with words that make her burn, her blood passionate for me.

85

I hate and love.
    And if you ask me why,
I have no answer, but I discern,
can feel, my senses rooted in eternal torture.

92

Lesbia, forever spitting fire at me, is never silent. And now
if Lesbia fails to love me, I shall die. Why
do I know in truth her passion burns for me? Because I am
    like her,
because I curse her endlessly. And still, O hear me gods,
I love her.

(tr. Horace Gregory)

From Sextus Propertius

I. vi

I am no ordinary coward, Tullus;
I do not fear the dangers of the seas.
I'd climb the Alps with you as my companion,
or voyage past the far Hesperides.
It's Cynthia's arms have robbed me of my valor;
I hear her weep, I watch her as she pales,
swearing the gods will leave her all forsaken—
I watch, I listen, and my courage fails.
Though she is mine, she will not let me take her;
she screams that if I leave her she will die.
Refusals, threats and tears—these are her weapons.
You could not face them, Tullus, nor can I.
What heart have I for Athens or for Asia?
I'd hear her words, shrieked out, half-heard, wind-snatched
across the widening waters, and I'd see her,
her face all bloodied where her nails have scratched.
You have your uncle's record to surpass, now—
like him the governor, you must seek the good.
You've never loved a woman. What you cherish
is patriotism, justice, brotherhood.
O but that's wise, that's safe, that's as it should be!
Never let loving make a fool of you.
I would not wish an enemy, much less Tullus,
the agonies that Cynthia puts me through.
Fortune has willed it so, that I should suffer,
obedient to the worst she may demand.
Well, men have died for love, they say, and gladly.
I shall be one of that immortal band.
I am not fit for warfare and its glories;
love's is the only war that I can wage.
But you, whatever fortune may befall you,
whatever honors come to you with age—
sea-captain or explorer, merchant, ruler
beloved by all his subjects near and far—
if, in those days, you think of me, remember:
I was born under an unlucky star.

I. xviii

Lonely and silent, here's a place for weeping;
only the West Wind moves among the leaves.
Here I may pour out sorrow, if the bare crags,
lonely themselves, keep faith with one who grieves.
Cynthia, tell me: what has made you scorn me?
when was the first time, Cynthia, you broke my heart?
A month ago I was the favored lover;
now, driven forth, I stand outside, apart.
Do I deserve this? has some magic changed you?
do you suspect I've turned to someone new?
No, no! come back, my fickle one; I'm faithful;
no girl will ever pass this door but you.
I should repay in bitterness my suffering,
yet, when I rage, my anger disappears
lest I should give you reason to be angry
or fill your heart with pain, your eyes with tears.
Or do you think I do not prove my passion
by tell-tale pallor, or an anguished face?
O let me call upon the trees for witness,
Pan's pine tree, or the beech—they know love's grace;
how often they have heard my crying Cynthia!
how deep I've carved your name upon their bark!
That doorway where I've wept knows how you've wronged me,
that doorway, closed against me, chill and dark.
When you were haughty, always I was humble,
silent although you stretched me on the rack—
and what return? a bed of rock to lie on,
and broken slumber on this rugged track.
The cries I cannot stifle—sea birds' voices,
screeching and shrill, must drown them all. And yet,
whatever you are, these woods still echo Cynthia.
It is your name these rocks will not forget.

II. iv

What's to do first? Forgive her sins against you;
asking her favor, know you'll be denied;
biting your fingernails, rage at unfairness;
stamp on the ground—but pocket all your pride.
I sleeked my hair (could vanity be vainer?)
and walked slow-paced and straight, to catch her eye.
My ills no sorceress, not even Medea,
could brew a cure for. Here's the reason why:
none sees the cause of it, the blow that's dealt us;
such griefs come to us by a secret path.
We seek no storm winds or their aftermath,
we walk abroad—and die without a warning.
No man is proof against this love, it seems.
What fortune tellers I have found were humbugs!
How many hags have riddled me my dreams!
A woman's love? My enemies may have it.
I wish my friends the love of some young boy.
From him no griefs; an easy tranquil journey
on little waves that bring no pain but joy.
Him you can soften with a single word;
die, and you leave her cold heart still unstirred.

How we rejoiced, my Cynthia and I,
thanking the gods who would not let us part!
The law's repealed at last, that threatening law
that might have riven heart from loving heart,
though Jove himself could not divide true lovers—
could Caesar? Caesar's glorious in war,
but what to love are all his conquered nations?
Cut off my head—I'd rather that fare more:
how could I leave this love to wed another,
and, husband to that other, pass your gate
nor turn back, blind with weeping, to this doorway,
knowing my loss, and knowing it too late?
And of what slumbers would those wedding trumpets
tell you? Their sound would turn into a knell.
I shall beget no sons to swell Rome's glory;
not of my sons shall Rome's historians tell.
But let me follow in your camp, my darling,
and I could bridle Castor's mighty horse—
they know me in the wilds beyond the Dnieper,
so my fame grows and widens in its course.
Let me be your one joy; you at my side,
I have no need of sons to feed my pride.

II. viii

She's torn from me, the girl I've loved so dearly
for years—and you, you tell me not to weep?
No enmity but love's can be so bitter.
Kill me—my hatred would not be so deep.
How can I bear to see another hold her?
She was so lately mine; is she no more?
All changes, loves not least, with the wheel's turning.
You win, you lose; it's always either-or.
The mightiest lords and leaders all are fallen;
the suns of Troy and Thebes are in eclipse
forever. Though for her my gifts, my poems,
I never heard I love you from her lips.

II. xii

Whoever first portrayed Love as life,
Would you not judge his skill beyond compare?
He saw the lack of wisdom in Love's life,
the bounty lost because of fretting care,
and with good reason gave Love windy wings
and made him flutter in the hearts of men—
the winds of chance toss men on shifting seas
and swing them hence and swing them back again.
And he was right to make Love's arrows barbed,
and sling the quiver ready to the hand:
Love's is an ambush no man can foresee
nor any human breast that wound withstand.
To me he's still the boy whose hurt I bear
but who, shorn of his wings, will fly no more—
here in my heart he lives, and in my blood
wages assiduous and unceasing war.
Why should you choose this shrivelled heart for home?
Shame on you! Seek your conquest otherwhere.
They are fair game who never felt your shaft—
what prize am I, a shadow thin as air?
Yet who would laud you, were that shadow lost?
My Muse is your renown, however slight.
Who else can praise so well my girl's dark eyes,
or say how soft her hands, her step how light?

Not even Agamemnon's joy was greater
when Troy was conquered with its treasure hoard;
not even Ulysses', docking at his homeland;
Electra's, with Orestes safe restored—
though she had mourned what she believed his ashes;
not Adriadne's, when the Cretan snares
were powerless over Theseus. . . . Their rejoicing
is mine. No, mine is greater even than theirs.
Last night has made me king, has made me hero:
make me immortal with another night!
Am I that drooping suppliant she scoffed at,
called a dry pool, made victim of her spite?
Whom does she meet no more with taunts and sarcasm?
who makes her run to do his bidding? I!
How could I take so long to learn her peace terms?
I groan to think of all those nights gone by.
A man in love, as I am, stumbles blindly,
missing the path that otherwise were plain.
Lovers, take heart: such blindness I've a cure for,
an easy formula—one word: Disdain.
Cold-shoulder her who scorns you, and, I promise,
in all that you have dreamed of you'll succeed.
Last night how many rivals begged for entrance!
Her head upon my heart, she did not heed.
O greatest victory, I move in triumph,
kings in my train and laurel for my head.
Venus, I pray you, let me deck your altars
and let this verse beneath my name be read:
These Are The Grateful Offerings Of Propertius,
Who For One Whole Night Shared His Mistress' Bed.
But all's not well yet. Will my ship come safely
to port, or will it founder close to shore?
If any fault of mine should change you, darling,
then may you find me dead before your door.

II. xvii

If you must lie to me about your lovers,
beguiling me, my blood is on your head.
Each night of solitude I sing my sorrows,
lying alone—and you in what man's bed?
Pity poor Tantalus, waist-deep in water
that shrinks whenever he would quench his thirst;
or Sisyphus who strains to push the boulder
up the long slope, and fails. Pity these cursed,
but pity even more the piteous lover—
lover with whom no wise man would change place.
I, once the king admitted and admired,
for ten days now I have not seen your face.
Bitch! I should find a rock, a cliff, to leap from,
or mix a poisonous drug and drink it down.
I cannot hurl my words at that closed doorway,
nor wander weeping through the moonlit town.

Yet I can't leave her, though I try it often.
Seeing how true I am, may she not soften?

III. xxiii

All my filled notebooks lost, and vanished with them
so much good writing—where could they have gone?
I've used them for so long now they've grown dingy;
no need for any seal set thereupon.
Rough drafts of notes, they kept love close in absence,
and kept me, absent, vivid to her eyes.
Plain things they were, no golden trimmings on them;
the wax was thin, the frame of no great size.
To any casual glance they'd have no value,
and yet they won for me some small success.
Sometimes she'd write to me on them: I'm angry.
What's your excuse for last night's tardiness?
You thought you'd find a prettier girl than this one?
You've spread more rumors that will do me wrong?
or, on a happier note: Come soon, my darling,
where love will make you welcome all night long.
Words from my lively chattering quick-witted Cynthia,
offering us long hours for love to fill—
and now some merchant tucks them in his ledger
or, on the back, scribbles his greasy bill!
There's a reward in gold for their returning—
who'd keep the trash when he could claim the prize?
Print the address—the Esquiline—down here, boy,
and post the notice to catch all men's eyes.

(tr. Constance Carrier)

From Ovid: The Metamorphoses

BOOK I: APOLLO AND DAPHNE

Though earth may not have willed catastrophe
The latest of new creatures was the serpent,
Even you, great Python of hillside and valley
Who haunt the deepest shadows in men's hearts!
Wherever the monster turned, green darkness fell
In winding paths through sacred grove and briar.
Then bright Apollo with his sun-tipped arrows
Whose swiftness stilled the flight of goat and deer
Aimed at the beast with darts that fell in showers.
So Python perished, but not until his wounds
Were black with blood and God Apollo's quiver
Almost spent. That is the reason why
Apollo's games are called the Pythian Feast,
In memory of the serpent's golden death,
In honor of the god's swift victory—
The Feast that brings fleet-footed, swift-riding
Youth garlands of oak leaf as they win the race.
This was before the laurel wreath became
Apollo's gift of grace in shrine and temple
Before he twined the green immortal laurel
Within the sunlight of his golden hair.

Apollo's first love was elusive Daphne,
The child of Peneus, kindly tyrant of the river,
Nor did the god pursue the girl by chance—
The cause was Cupid's anger at Apollo:
Still heated by his conquest of the snake,
Phoebus saw Cupid wind a tight-strung bow,
"Who is this lecherous child," said he, "who plays
With weapons and is not a man? The bow
Was made for me; I am the one who kills
A worthy enemy, wild beasts—and look at
Great Python wallowing in blood; his body
Covers half the countryside. Your business
Is not to play with arrows, but set afire
Your little torch that guides unwary lovers."
The child of Venus glanced at flush Apollo:

"Your arrows may be murder to us all,
But mine shall pierce your veins: as much
As mortals are less than the divine, so
Your poor glory is less than my poor skill."
With that he raised his wings and in quick air
He found a shaded ledge on high Parnassus;
There carefully he made a choice of arrows—
Two darts that were of opposite persuasion,
One, like a golden spear, was sharp as fire,
And is love's fire in the flesh, the other,
Heavy as boredom, dull as lead, he plunged
At a single stroke into white Daphne's breast.
Then Cupid aimed at Phoebus, and love's arrow
With fire of lightning pierced his bones;
Apollo walked as in a tower of flames.
As Phoebus burned with love young Daphne fled
As though she feared love's name, as if she were
The wraith of virgin Phoebe, huntress and child
Who trapped small creatures of the bushbank fen,
And ran with floating hair through green-deep forest;
Nor would she hear of lovers or of men,
Nor cared for promise of a wedding day,
Nor Hymen's night of love. Time and again
Old Peneus complained, "Where is my son-in-law,
Daughter, where have you hidden my grandchildren?"
As though the wedding torch were sight of evil
Pale Daphne flushed at every thought of it,
And hid her face against her father's shoulder
And pleading with her arms around his neck
Said, "Father, make me an eternal virgin.
Do what Diana's father did for her."
Peneus agreed, but your enchantments, Daphne,
Had greater powers than a father's will,
Nor could your prayers undo a beauty's charm.
At one look Phoebus loved her; as he gazed,
"Daphne," he thought, "is mine," but did not think
His prophecy might fail him—his hopes, desires
Had outpaced all the Delian oracles;
Then as September fields of wheat and straw
Take fire from a careless traveller's torch
Left smouldering in the wind that wakes the dawn,
So did Apollo's heart break into flames,
The sterile fires that feed on empty hopes.
And while he gazed at Daphne's floating hair

That fell in tendrils at her throat and forehead
He thought, "What if that fair head wore a crown?"
He looked into her eyes and saw the stars.
Though staring does not satisfy desire,
His eyes praised all they saw—her lips, her fingers,
Her hands, her naked arms from wrist to shoulder;
And what they did not see they thought the best.
Yet she ran from him swifter than light air
That turns to nothingness as we pursue it,
Nor did she stop to hear Apollo calling:
"O daughter of the deep green-shadowed River,
Who follows you is not your enemy;
The lamb runs from the wolf, the deer from lion,
The trembling-feathered dove flies from the eagle
Whose great wings cross the sky—such is your flight
While mine is love's pursuit. Rest where time waits
But where you vanish the way is rough; briar
And thorn and fallen rock make wounds that bleed,
And green pits open where swift unwary fall.
And I who follow am neither pain nor death;
Then walk with me and ask me who I am.
Surely my home is not in mountain passes,
Nor am I shepherd or wild-haired stable boy.
O ignorant, unknowing, thoughtless child
Who runs in darkness—and from whom? from me?
Jove is my father and I am lord of Delphi;
My temples stand at Claros, Patara,
And beyond the cities, glimmering Tenebros,
Enchanted island of the eastern seas.
Where caves and temples speak you hear my voices,
The past, the present, and the yet to come;
My lyre sounds the soul of harmony;
My arrows never fail—and yet one arrow
More certain of its aim than mine wakes fire
Behind the chambers of an indifferent heart.
And if you wait, learn more: I am physician,
The good physician of magic in clever herbs
And artful grasses; yet herbs are feeble cures,
Unhealthy diet for one who falls in love,
Nor can physician cure himself—"

    As Daphne ran
Phoebus had more to say, and she, distracted,
In flight, in fear, wind flowing through her dress

And her wild hair—she grew more beautiful
The more he followed her and saw wind tear
Her dress and the short tunic that she wore,
The girl a naked wraith in wilderness.
And as they ran young Phoebus saved his breath
For greater speed to close the race, to circle
The spent girl in an open field, to harry
The chase as greyhound races hare,
His teeth, his black jaws glancing at her heels.
The god by grace of hope, the girl, despair,
Still kept their increasing pace until his lips
Breathed at her shoulder; and almost spent,
The girl saw waves of a familiar river,
Her father's home, and in a trembling voice
Called, "Father, if your waters still hold charms
To save your daughter, cover with green earth
This body I wear too well," and as she spoke
A soaring drowsiness possessed her; growing
In earth she stood, white thighs embraced by climbing
Bark, her white arms branches, her fair head swaying
In a cloud of leaves; all that was Daphne bowed
In the stirring of the wind, the glittering green
Leaf twined within her hair and she was laurel.

Even now Phoebus embraced the lovely tree
Whose heart he felt still beating in its side;
He stroked its branches, kissed the sprouting bark,
And as the tree still seemed to sway, to shudder
At his touch, Apollo whispered, "Daphne,
Who cannot be my wife must be the seal,
The sign of all I own, immortal leaf
Twined in my hair as hers, and by this sign
My constant love, my honour shall be shown:
When Roman captains home from victory
Ride with the Legions up Capitoline,
Their heads will shine with laurels and wherever
The Augustus sets his gates, plain or frontier,
Or Roman city wall, the bronze oak leaf
And the green-pointed laurel shall guard the portal
And grace the Roman crown." As Phoebus spoke,
The laurel shook her branches and seemed to bow
A timid blessing on her lover's pleasure.

BOOK II: JOVE AND EUROPA

After the god had punished Cecrops' daughter
For blasphemy in deed and word and soul,
He left Athenian country far below him
And flew to heaven on his outstretched wings.
Where to the highest place his father drew him
In confidence, nor did he speak of love,
But said, "Dear son, the best of messengers,
And loyal to every lively whim of mine,
Slip down to earth at once into that land
Which views your mother's star from its left side;
(It is the place its countrymen call Sidon).
Once there, drive the king's cattle to seashore;
You'll find them grazing near the mountaintop."
No sooner said than done: as Jove commanded,
The cattle marched from mountain to the beach
Where the king's daughter had a common playground
With her Tyrian girls, Royal dignity
And love are seldom known to go to bed
Together—therefore the Father
Of all Gods whose right hand held a three-pronged
Thunderbolt, whose slightest nod was earthquake
Up to heaven, dropped his royal sceptre and
Became a bull. Speaking their tongue, he moved
Among the cows; more beautiful than they
Or other bulls, he strolled spring grasses,
White as the snow untouched by Southern rains
Or footprint on the ground, huge, silky muscles
At his neck and silvered dewlaps hanging,
Small horns as white as if a sculptor's hand
Had cut them out of pearl. And no one feared
His look; forehead and eye were gracefully
Benign. He was so portly, beautiful,
So easy, Agenor's daughter gazed at
Him in wonder. At first she was afraid
(Though he seemed gentle) to touch the creature—
Then she went to him with a gift of daisies
To his snow-white lips. He was all joy, tasting
The future as he kissed her hands, nor could he
Straightly control his love: he danced the grasses
And rolled his whiteness into golden sands.
Then when she came less shy, he gave his breast
To her caressing hands and let her garland
Even his dainty horns with new-plucked flowers.

The princess, innocent on whom she sat,
Climbed to his back; slowly the god stepped out
Into the shallows of the beach and with
False-footed softness took to sea, swimming
Against full tide, the girl his captured prize;
She, fearful, turned to shoreward, set one hand
On his broad back, the other held one horn,
Her dress behind her fluttered in the wind.

BOOK III: ECHO AND NARCISSUS

Throughout the cities of Boeotia
Tiresias had become a famous man;
Those who came to him for advice could not
Deny the power, his wit, in prophecy;
The first test of his power to tell truth
Came from Liriope, a water-lady
Whom Cephisus raped within a winding brook
And nearly drowned her. Then in her due time
The pretty girl gave birth to a sweet child,
A son so charming even as a baby,
That he inspired girls with thoughts of love—
She called the boy Narcissus. When she asked
Tiresias how long her child would live—
To great old age? the prophet answered, "Only
If never he comes to know himself." Then for
A long time after this his prophecy
Seemed vain, and yet what finally happened
Proved it true: Narcissus' death, the way he died,
And his odd love. For when Narcissus reached
His sixteenth year he seemed to be a boy
As much as man; both boys and girls looked to him
To make love, and yet that slender figure
Of proud Narcissus had little feeling
For either boys or girls. One day when he
Had shied a nervous deer into a net,
A girl with a queer voice stood gazing at him—
Echo, who could not check her tongue while talking,
Nor could she speak till someone spoke to her.

In those days Echo was far more than voice;
She had a body and, though garrulous,
No further gifts of speech than now: in short,
The art of taking, from much said, the last
few words. Juno had made her so; in time
Gone by when Juno might have startled

Jove in the arms of girls on mountainsides,
Echo kept Juno in long conversations
Until the girls had run away. When Juno
Discovered this, she said, "That tongue which has
Deceived me shall make nothing but the poor
Brief noises of the fewest words." Therefore
It came about that Echo's speech was cut,
Yet she retains the last sounds that she hears,
And says them back again to those around her.
The day she saw the wandering Narcissus
Stroll through the forest, secretly she glided,
Fired with love, to follow him; and as she
Came closer to his side, the very source
Of flames increased her heat; she was as sulphur
At the tip of torches, leaping to fire
When another flame leans toward it. She longed
To lure him with soft words, with girlish prayers.
But being what she was she could not make
Sounds come; she had to wait until she heard
Words said, then follow them in her own voice.
Meanwhile Narcissus, strayed from all his friends,
Began to shout, "Is anybody here?"
"Here," Echo answered, and the wondering boy
Looked far around him and cried louder, "Come."
"Come," she called after him. He glanced behind,
Saw no one there, then shouted, "Why run from me?"
And only heard the same words follow him.
Then he stood still, held by deceptive sounds;
"Here we shall meet," he said, and Echo never
Replied more eagerly—"Here we shall meet."
To make those words come true, she slipped beyond
The shelter of the trees to throw her arms
Around the boy she would embrace. Yet he
Ran from her, crying, "No, you must not touch—
Go, take your hands away, may I be dead
Before you throw your fearful chains around me."
"O fearful chains around me," Echo said,
And then no more. So she was turned away
To hide her face, her lips, her guilt among the trees,
Even their leaves, to haunt caves of the forest,
To feed her love on melancholy sorrow
Which, sleepless, turned her body to a shade,
First pale and wrinkled, then a sheet of air,
Then bones, which some say turned to thin-worn rocks;
And last her voice remained. Vanished in forest,

Far from her usual walks on hills and valleys,
She's heard by all who call; her voice has life.

The way Narcissus had betrayed frail Echo.
Now swift, now shy, so he had played with all:
Girls of the rivers, women of the mountains,
With boys and men. Until one boy, love-sick
And left behind, raised prayers to highest heaven:
"O may he love himself alone," he cried,
"And yet fail in that great love." The curse was heard
By wakeful Nemesis. Deep in the forest
Was a pool, well-deep and silver-clear, where
Never a shepherd came, nor goats, nor cattle;
Nor leaf, nor beast, nor bird fell to its surface.
Nourished by water, grass grew thick around it,
And over it dark trees had kept the sun
From ever shedding warmth upon the place.
Here spent Narcissus, weary of the hunt
And sick with heat, fell to the grass, charmed by
The bright well and its greenery. He bent
To drink, to dissipate his thirst, yet as he
Drank another thirst rose up: enraptured
Beauty caught his eyes that trapped him;
He loved the image that he thought was shadow,
And looked amazed at what he saw—his face.
Fixed, bending over it, he could not speak,
Himself as though cut from Parian marble.
Flat on the grass he lay to look deep, deeper
Into two stars that were his eyes, at hair
Divine as Bacchus' hair, as bright Apollo's,
At boyish beauty of ivory neck and shoulder,
At face, flushed as red flowers among white,
Enchanted by the charms which were his own.
Himself the worshipped and the worshipper,
He sought himself and was pursued, wooed, fired
By his own heat of love. Again, again
He tried to kiss the image in the well;
Again, again his arms embraced the silver
Elusive waters where his image shone;
And he burned for it while the gliding error
Betrayed his eyes. O foolish innocent!
Why try to grasp at shadows in their flight?
What he had tried to hold resided nowhere,

For had he turned away, it fell to nothing:
His love was cursed. Only the glancing mirror
Of reflections filled his eyes, a body
That had no being of its own, a shade
That came, stayed, left with him—if he could leave it.

    Neither desire of food or sleep could lure
Him from the well, but flat upon the grasses
There he lay, fixed by the mirage of his eyes
To look until sight failed. And then, half turning,
Raised arms to dark trees over him and cried,
"O trees, O forest, has anyone been cursed
With love like mine? O you who know the ways
Of many lovers in your shaded groves,
Was there at any time that long past,
The centuries you knew, one who is spent,
Wasted like this? I am entranced, enchanted
By what I see, yet it eludes me, error
Or hope becomes the thing I love; and now
With every hour increases sorrow; nor sea,
Nor plain, nor city walls, nor mountain ranges
Keeps us apart. Only this veil of water.
So thin the veil we almost touch each other,
Then come to me no matter who you are,
O lovely boy, why do you glide from me,
Where do you vanish when I come to meet you?
My youth, my beauty cannot be denied,
For girls have loved me and your tempting glances
Tell me of friendship in your eyes. Even as
I reach, your arms almost embrace me, and as
I smile, you smile again at me; weeping
I've seen great tears flow down your face; I bend
My head toward you, you nod at me, and I
Believe that from the movement of your lips
(Though nothing's heard) you seem to answer me.
Look! I am he; I've loved within the shadow
Of what I am, and in that love I burn,
I light the flames and feel their fires within;
Then what am I to do? Am I the lover
Or beloved? Then why make love? Since I
Am what I long for, then my riches are
So great they make me poor. O may I fall
Away from my own body—and this is odd

From any lover's lips—I would my love
Would go away from me. And now love drains
My life, look! I am dying at life's prime
Nor have I fear of death which ends my trials,
Yet wish my lover had a longer life,
If not, we two shall perish in one breath."

He spoke and half mad faced the self-made image.
Tears stirred the pool to waves, the wavering features
Dimmed in darkest waters. As he saw them flicker
He cried, "Where are you going? Stay with me;
O cruelest lover come, nor leave me here;
It may be fate for me to look at love
And yet not touch it, but in that deep gaze
Increase unhappy love to misery."
Then in his agony he tore his dress
And beat his naked breast with his pale hands.
As apples ripen, some parts white, some red,
As growing grapes take on a purple shade,
Narcissus' breast put on these darkening colours;
And when he saw them—for the pool had cleared—
He could endure no more, but as wax turns
To liquid in mild heat, as autumn frost
Changes to dew at morning, so did Narcissus
Wear away with love, drained, fading in the heat
Of secret fires. No longer were his colours
Gold, white, and red and that vitality
His beauty showed, but something less, scarcely
The boy whom Echo loved too well. Yet when
She saw him, and though still annoyed, resentful,
She felt a touch of pity at the sight,
So when he sighed "Eheu," "Eheu," said she,
And as his hands struck at his breast and shoulders,
So she repeated these weak sounds of grief.
As gazing down the well, his last words were:
"O darling boy whose love was my undoing,"
And all the grove resounded with their saying.
Then with his last "Good-bye," "Good-bye," said Echo.
At this he placed his head deep in cool grasses
While death shut fast the eyes that shone with light
At their own lustre. As he crossed the narrows
Of darkest hell he saw the floating image
Of his lost shade within the Stygian waters.
His sisters of the rivers beat their breasts

And shaved their heads in sorrow for their brother,
Nor were the sisters of the forest silent,
But filled the air with grief which Echo carried.
As they built up his pyre and waved their torches
Across his bier, they searched; his body vanished.
They saw a flower of gold with white-brimmed petals.

BOOK IV: MARS AND VENUS

The story ended, but a moment later
Leuconoe began—her sisters silent:
"Even the Sun whose light rules all the stars
Has known love's kingdom; we shall tell of it.
Since he was always first to see what happened
He was the first to find that Mars and Venus
Took pleasure with each other, which was wrong.
Amazed at what he saw, he spoke to Vulcan,
Husband of Venus and great Juno's son,
And told him where he caught them in the act.
Then Vulcan's mind went dark; he dropped his work
And turned at once to subtle craftsmanship,
To make a net so light, so delicate,
So thinly woven of fine-tempered bronze
The casual, glancing eye would never see it—
Less visible than sleekest threads of wool
Or nets that spiders hang from tallest beams.
He made it so it yielded at each touch,
Each trembling gesture or the slightest movement,
Then draped it as a sheet on his wife's bed.
So shrewdly was it made that when the goddess
Took to her bed within her lover's arms,
Both were caught up and held within the net.
Then Vulcan, fisherman, threw wide his doors,
Which shone in burnished shafts of ivory,
And called the other gods to see his catch,
To see how lovers act within their chains.
One god remarked that he half envied Mars,
While Vulcan's bedroom shook with godly laughter:
For many years this tale was told in heaven . . . "

BOOK X: PYGMALION

"Pygmalion knew these women all too well;
Even if he closed his eyes, his instincts told him
He'd better sleep alone. He took to art,
Ingenious as he was, and made a creature
More beautiful than any girl on earth,
A miracle of ivory in a statue,
So charming that it made him fall in love.
Her face was life itself; she was a darling—
And yet too modest to permit advances
Which showed his art had artful touches in it,
The kind of art that swept him off his feet;
He stroked her arms, her face, her sides, her shoulder.
Was she alive or not? He could not tell.
He kissed her; did her lips respond to his?
And felt a living whiteness move; then, frightened,
He hoped he had not stained that perfect beauty.
He whispered at her—look, he brought her toys,
Small gifts that girls delight to wear, to gaze at,
Pet birds and shells and semi-precious stones,
White lilies, flowers of a thousand colours,
The amber tears wept by Heliades.
He dressed her like a queen, rings on her fingers,
Or diamonds and gold or glancing rubies;
A shining collar at her throat, pearls at her ears,
And golden chains encircling her small breasts.
All these were beautiful enough, yet greater beauty
Shone from her nakedness in bed; he called her
His bride, his wife, the fair white creature sleeping
On cloth of purple, as if she shared his dreams,
Her head at rest upon a feathered pillow.

"Meanwhile the Feast of Venus had arrived
And all of Cyprus joined in celebration:
Golden-horned cattle lay at smoke-wreathed altars,
Blood pouring from white throats in sacrifice
In honour of a blessed holiday.
Pygmalion, after paying his devotions,
Began a prayer, then shyness overcame him;
He whispered, 'May the very Gods in Heaven
Give me a wife'—he could not say outright,
'Give me the girl I made.' He stammered,
Then went on: 'But someone like—'
He cleared his throat, then said, 'Give me a lady

Who is as lovely as my work of art.'
The prayer was scarcely heard, yet golden Venus
(Who on that day had come to join the feast)
Was well aware of what Pygmalion longed for:
Three times his altar burned in whitest fire;
Three times its flames leaped floating into air,
Six friendly omens of her good intentions.
Then he ran home to see, to touch again
The ivory image that his hands contrived,
And kissed the sleeping lips, now soft, now warm,
Then touched her breasts and cupped them in his hands;
They were as though ivory had turned to wax
And wax to life, yielding, yet quick with breath.
Pygmalion, half-dazed, lost in his raptures,
And half in doubt, afraid his senses failed him,
Touched her again and felt his hopes come true,
The pulse-beat stirring where he moved his hands.
Then, as if words could never say enough,
He poured a flood of praise to smiling Venus.
He kissed the girl until she woke beneath him.
Her eyes were shy; she flushed; yet her first look
Saw at one glance his face and Heaven above it.
Venus came down to be their guest at wedding
And blessed them both. Less than a year went by—
Scarcely the ninth moon filled her slender crescent;
A girl was born to them—Paphos they called her,
And from that child a harbour takes it name . . . "

BOOK X: VENUS AND ADONIS

"Time slipped away: there's nothing more elusive
Than Time in flight, more swift in flight than he
Who steals our years and months, our days and hours.
Son of a sister whom he never saw,
Son of a grandfather who cursed his being,
Child of a tree, Adonis grew to boyhood—
And lovelier than any man on earth.
When Venus looked at him, his mother's guilt
Seemed like an old and half-forgotten story,
And on that day as Eros stooped to kiss her,
His quiver slipped, an arrow scratched her breast;
She thrust her son aside and shook her head
While that swift cut went deeper than she knew.
She found Adonis beautiful and mortal

And lost her taste for old immortal places:
The shores of Cythera, the sea-green harbours
Where Paphos floated like a jewel-set finger,
Cnidos, the rocks where wheeling fishes spawn,
Even Amathus streaked in rich gold and bronze,
And she was bored with living in the skies.
On Earth she took Adonis for an airing,
An arm around his waist, and thought this better
Than golden afternoons on Mount Olympus.
Before she met him she used to lie on grasses
To rest in shade and wreath herself with flowers,
But now she walked abroad through brush and briar,
Climbed rocks and hills, and, looking like Diana,
She wore short dresses, poised as a mistress out
To lead the hunt—yet she sought harmless game,
The nervous rabbit and high-antlered deer.
Her rule was to keep shy of savage brutes—
The lunging boar, the wolf, the bear, the lion—
All those who lived by killing men and cattle,
Who smelled of blood. Adonis had her warning,
If any warning could have held him back.
She told him, 'Save your valour for the timid—
The wild and large are much too wild for you;
My dear, remember that sweet Venus loves you,
And if you walk in danger, so does she.
Nature has armed her monsters to destroy you—
Even your valour would be grief to me.
What Venus loves—the young, the beautiful—
Mean less than nothing to huge, hungry creatures
Who tear and bite and have wide, staring eyes:
The boar whose crooked teeth are lightning flashes,
The stormy lion and his raging jaws.
They have my fears and hates; I know them well.'
And when Adonis asked her why, she said,
'I'll tell you how I know: there is a story
That has a fearful end, and there are wonders
For you to hear. I've walked too far today,
At your quick pace. Look, there's a willow tree
And under it a bed of grass and clover;
We'll have our rest within that charming shade.'
They slipped to earth, her head upon his breast,
And when from time to time she sought for words,
She raised her face to his and kissed his lips . . . "

BOOK X: ORPHEUS AND EURYDICE

When his farewells were said at Iphis' wedding,
Hymen leaped into space toward blue uncharted skies,
His golden-amber colours gliding up,
Till he sailed over Thrace where Orpheus hailed him
(But not entirely to his advantage)
To bless another wedding celebration.
Though Hymen came to help him at the feast
And waved his torch, its fires guttered out
In coiling smoke that filled the eyes with tears.
Then on the morning after, things went wrong:
While walking carelessly through sun-swept grasses,
Like Spring herself, with all her girls-in-waiting,
The bride stepped on a snake; pierced by his venom,
The girl tripped, falling, stumbled into Death.
Her bridegroom, Orpheus, poet of the hour,
And pride of Rhadope, sang loud his loss
To everyone on earth. When this was done,
His wailing voice, his lyre, and himself
Came weaving through the tall gates of Taenarus
Down to the world of Death and flowing Darkness
To tell the story of his grief again.
He took his way through crowds of drifting shades
Who had escaped their graves to hear his music
And stood at last where Queen Persephone
Joined her unyielding lord to rule that desert
Which had been called their kingdom. Orpheus
Tuned up his lyre and cleared his throat to sing:
"O King and Queen of this vast Darkness where
All who are born of Earth at last return,
I cannot speak half flattery, half lies;
I have not come, a curious, willing guest
To see the streets of Tartarus wind in Hell,
Nor have I come to tame Medusa's children
Three-throated beasts with wild snakes in their hair.
My mission is to find Eurydice,
A girl whose thoughts were innocent and gay,
Yet tripped upon a snake who struck his poison
Into her veins—then her short walk was done.
However much I took her loss serenely,
A god called Love had greater strength than I;
I do not know how well he's known down here,
But up on Earth his name's on every tongue,

And if I'm to believe an ancient rumour,
A dark king took a princess to his bed,
A child more beautiful than any queen;
They had been joined by Love. So at your mercy,
And by the eternal Darkness that surrounds us,
I ask you to unspin the fatal thread
Too swiftly run, too swiftly cut away,
That was my bride's brief life. Hear me, and know
Another day, after our stay on Earth,
Or swift or slow, we shall be yours forever,
Speeding at last to one eternal kingdom—
Which is our one direction and our home—
And yours the longest reign mankind has known.
When my Eurydice has spent her stay on Earth,
The child, a lovely woman in your arms,
Then she'll return and you may welcome her.
But for the present I must ask a favour;
Let her come back to me to share my love,
Yet if the Fates say 'No,' here shall I stay—
Two deaths in one—my death as well as hers."

    Since these pathetic words were sung to music
Even the blood-drained ghosts of Hell fell weeping:
Tantalus no longer reached toward vanished waves
And Ixion's wheel stopped short, charmed by the spell;
Vultures gave up their feast on Tityus' liver
And cocked their heads to stare; fifty Belides
Stood gazing while their half-filled pitchers emptied,
And Sisyphus sat down upon his stone.
Then, as the story goes, the raging Furies
Grew sobbing-wet with tears. Neither the queen
Nor her great lord of Darkness could resist
The charms of Orpheus and his matchless lyre.
They called Eurydice, and there among
The recent dead she came, still hurt and limping
At their command. They gave him back his wife
With this proviso: that as he led her up
From where Avernus sank into a valley,
He must not turn his head to look behind him.
They climbed a hill through clouds, pitch-dark and
    gloomy,
And as they neared the surface of the Earth,
The poet, fearful that she'd lost her way,
Glanced backward with a look that spoke his love—

Then saw her gliding into deeper darkness,
As he reached out to hold her, she was gone;
He had embraced a world of emptiness.
This was her second death—and yet she could not
    blame him
(Was not his greatest fault great love for her?)
She answered him with one last faint "Good-bye,"
An echo of her voice from deep Avernus.

When Orpheus saw his wife go down to Death,
Twice dead, twice lost, he stared like someone dazed.
He seemed to be like him who saw the fighting
Three-headed Dog led out by Hercules
In chains, a six-eyed monster spitting bile;
The man was paralyzed and fear ran through him
Until his very body turned to stone.
Or rather, Orpheus, was not unlike
Lethaea's husband, who took on himself
The sin of being proud of his wife's beauty,
Of which that lady bragged too much and long,
Yet since their hearts were one (in their opinion)
They changed to rocks where anyone may see them
Hold hands and kiss where Ida's fountains glitter.
Soon Orpheus went "melancholy-mad":
As often as old Charon pushed him back,
He begged, he wept to cross the Styx again.
Then for a week he sat in rags and mud,
Nor ate nor drank; he lived on tears and sorrow.
He cried against the gods of black Avernus
And said they made him suffer and go wild;
Then, suddenly, as if his mood had shifted,
He went to Thrace and climbed up windy Haemus.

Three times the year had gone through waves of
    Pisces,
While Orpheus refused to sleep with women;
Whether this meant he feared bad luck in marriage,
Or proved him faithful to Eurydice,
No one can say, yet women followed him
And felt insulted when he turned them out.
Meanwhile he taught the men of Thrace the art
Of making love to boys and showed them that
Such love affairs renewed their early vigour,
The innocence of youth, the flowers of spring.

One day while walking down a little hill
He sloped upon a lawn of thick green grasses,
A lovely place to rest—but needed shade.
But when the poet, great-grandson of the gods,
Sat down to sing and touched his golden lyre,
There the cool grasses waves beneath green shadows,
For trees came crowding where the poet sang,
The silver poplar and the bronze-leaved oak,
The swaying lina, beechnut, maiden-laurel,
Delicate hazel and spear-making ash,
The shining silver fir, the ilex leaning
Its flower-weighted head, sweet-smelling fir,
The shifting-coloured maple and frail willow
Whose branches trail where gliding waters flow;
Lake-haunted lotus and the evergreening boxwood,
Thin tamarisk and the myrtle of two colours,
Viburnum with its darkly shaded fruit.
And with them came the slender-footed ivy,
Grapevine and vine-grown elms and mountain ash,
The deeply wooded spruce, the pink arbutus,
The palm whose leaves are signs of victory,
And the tall pine, beloved of Cybele
Since Attis her loyal priest stripped off his manhood,
And stood sexless and naked as that tree.

(tr. Horace Gregory)

From Petronius: Satyricon

Suddenly Psyche sidled up giggling, and whispered something into Quartilla's ear. "A splendid idea," said Quartilla, "I can't imagine a more opportune time for deflowering our little Pannychis." Immediately a rather pretty little girl—the same one who had come with Quartilla to our rooms—was led out. I doubt that she could have been more than seven, but with the exception of myself everybody present applauded the idea and demanded that the marriage be consummated instantly. I was shocked, however, and pointed out that Giton, a very bashful boy, could hardly be expected to undergo such drudgery yet. Besides, I protested, the girl was much too young to be assuming a woman's position.

"Pish," snorted Quartilla. "Is she any younger than I was when I had my first man? May Juno strike me dead if I can ever remember being a virgin. When I was a little girl, I played ducks and drakes with the little boys; as I got bigger, I applied myself to bigger boys, until I reached my present age—whence I think the proverb arose, she'll bear the bull that bore the calf." Fearing that Giton might suffer something still worse if I refused, I rose reluctantly to help with the ceremony. Psyche placed a saffron veil on the little girl's head, while a whole troop of drunken women, led by the eunuch with a blazing torch, marched off to prepare the room for this travesty of marriage. Quartilla, flushed and excited by the gross obscenity of the whole affair, took Giton by the hand and led him into the bedroom.

In point of fact the boy made no objection and even the little girl appeared quite unmoved by the notion of being a bride. Finally the door was shut, the bolts shot, and we all took up our positions around the door. Then Quartilla, standing in the front row, treacherously cut a slit in the panel and peeked with lecherous curiosity at their innocent childish play. With a gentle caress she drew me to the chink to watch too, and since our faces were often close together, kept turning her lips to me and stealing kisses.

XXII: RESTORED

"There are other gods still more powerful," I explained, "and it is they who have made me a man once more. Mercury himself, the god who guides our unborn souls to the light and leads the dead to hell, has taken pity on me and given me back that power which an angry hand once cut away. Look at me and tell me whether Protesilaus or any of those ancient heroes was ever more blessed by heaven than I am now." With that, I lifted my tunic and displayed myself in my erected glory. Gaping with astonishment and awe, utterly incapable of believing his eyes, he reached out his shaking hands and caressed that huge pledge of heaven's favor. . . .

(tr. William Arrowsmith)

From The Greek Anthology

Restless and discontent
I lie awake all night long.
And as I drowse in the dawn,
The swallows stir in the eaves,
And wake me weeping again.
I press my eyes close tight, but
Your face rises before me.
O birds, be quiet with
Your tittering accusations.
I did not cut that dead girl's tongue.
Go weep for her lover in the hills,
Cry by the hoopoe's nest in the rocks.
Let me sleep for a while, and dream
I lie once more in my girl's arms.

AGATHIAS SCHOLASTICOS
(tr. Kenneth Rexroth)

I have two sicknesses, Love
And Poverty. Poverty
I can stand, but the fever
Of Love is unbearable.

ANONYMOUS
(tr. Kenneth Rexroth)

I know I am poor,
Neither do I have to be reminded
Of my own name or
The day of the week.
All your bitterness will get us nowhere.
Wash the anchovies,
While I pour the wine.
Naked and drunk, we'll find riches in bed.

ANONYMOUS
(tr. Kenneth Rexroth)

Didyme waved her wand at me.
I am utterly enchanted.
The sight of her beauty makes me
Melt like wax before the fire. What
Is the difference if she is black?
So is coal, but alight, it shines like roses.

ASKLEPIADES
(*tr. Kenneth Rexroth*)

Get drunk, my boy, don't weep, you're
Not the only prisoner
Of love. Plenty of people
Are stuck all over with the
Barbed arrows of lust. Don't
Grovel. You're still alive.
Drink your liquor straight. Drink. Time
Is wasting. We may not be here at bedtime. Drink. Soon
Enough and long enough,
You'll find time for sleeping.

ASKLEPIADES
(*tr. Kenneth Rexroth*)

Lysidike dedicates
To you, Kypris, her jockey's
Spur, the golden prickle she
Wore on her beautiful leg.
Upside down, she broke many
Horses, yet her own bottom
Was never reddened, she had
Such a skillful seat that she
Always came first in the race.
Now she hangs her weapon in
The midst of your golden gate.

ASKLEPIADES
(*tr. Kenneth Rexroth*)

What are you saving it for?
When you get to Hell you'll find
Nobody there to love you, girl.
The fun of love is for the
Living. Dead virgins are just
Dust and ashes like us all.

ASKLEPIADES
(*tr. Kenneth Rexroth*)

Your flatteries are boring,
And your coquetries painful.
I am not godlike, and I
Am extremely impatient.
I am not going to turn
Into a bull or a swan,
Let alone a bufflehead,
Like cuckold Amphitryon.
Take off your clothes and lie down,
Or I shall get me a girl
Who wants a human lover.

BASSOS
(tr. Kenneth Rexroth)

In the Spring the quince and the
Pomegranate bloom in the
Sacred Park of the Maidens,
And the vine tendril curls in
The shade of the downy vine leaf.
But for me Love never sleeps.
He scorches me like a blaze
Of lightning and he shakes me
To the roots like a storm out of
Thrace, and he overwhelms my heart
With black frenzy and seasickness.

IBYKOS
(tr. Kenneth Rexroth)

THE ADVANTAGES OF LEARNING

I am a man with no ambitions
And few friends, wholly incapable
Of making a living, growing no
Younger, fugitive from some just doom.
Lonely, ill-clothed, what does it matter?
At midnight I make myself a jug
Of hot white wine and cardamon seeds.
In a torn grey robe and old beret,
I sit in the cold writing poems,
Drawing nudes on the crooked margins,
Copulating with sixteen year old
Nymphomaniacs of my imagination.

MARTIAL
(tr. Kenneth Rexroth)

You are the most beautiful
Girl there ever was or will be.
And you are the vilest girl
There ever was or will be.
O Catulla, how I wish
You had less beauty or more shame.

MARTIAL
(tr. Kenneth Rexroth)

I swear by desire
I would rather hear
Your voice than the sound
Of Apollo's lyre.

MELEAGROS
(tr. Kenneth Rexroth)

"Nothing is sweeter than love.
Every bliss takes second place.
Even honey I spit out of
My mouth." I, Nossis, say this,
"If any girl is unkissed
By love, she cannot tell what
Sort of flowers roses are."

NOSSIS
(*tr. Kenneth Rexroth*)

I have sworn ten thousand times
To make no more epigrams.
Every ass is my enemy now.
But when I look at your face,
The old sickness overcomes me.

PALLADAS
(*tr. Kenneth Rexroth*)

Eros has changed his quiver
For the fangs of Kerberos,
And I am hydrophobiac.
The sea smells of her body.
Her skirts rustle in the stream.
I go blind staggering drunk
With the very taste of wine
That calls back her sleep drugged lips.

PAULOS SILENTIARIOS
(*tr. Kenneth Rexroth*)

You're right, Lais' smile is sweet,
And the tears that drop from her
Fluttering eyelids are sweeter still.
Yesterday she leaned over me
And rested her head upon
My shoulder and sighed a long
Sigh. She wept as I kissed her
And tears fell from those dewy springs
And wet our mingled lips. And when
I asked her why she cried she
Said, "I am afraid you will
Leave me. You are all liars."

PAULOS SILENTIARIOS
(tr. Kenneth Rexroth)

Fornication is a filthy business,
The briefest form of lechery,
And the most boring, once you're satisfied.
So let's not rush blindly upon it,
Like cows in rut.
That's the way passion wilts
And the fire goes out.
But so and so, feasting without end,
Lie together kissing each other.
It's a lazy shameless thing,
Delights, has delighted, always will delight,
And never ends, but constantly begins again.

PETRONIUS
(tr. Kenneth Rexroth)

Doing, a filthy pleasure is, and short;
And done, we straight repent us of the sport:
Let us not then rush blindly on unto it;
Like lustful beasts, that only know to do it:
For lust will languish, and that heat decay.
But thus, thus, keeping endless holiday,
Let us together closely lie and kiss,
There is no labour, nor no shame in this;
This hath pleased, doth please, and long will please; never
Can this decay, but is beginning ever.

PETRONIUS
(tr. Ben Jonson)

GOOD GOD, WHAT A NIGHT THAT WAS

Good God, what a night that was,
The bed was so soft, and how we clung,
Burning together, lying this way and that,
Our uncontrollable passions
Flowing through our mouths.
If I could only die that way,
I'd say goodbye to the business of living.

PETRONIUS
(tr. Kenneth Rexroth)

I had just gone to bed
And begun to enjoy the first
Stillness of the night,
And sleep was slowly
Overcoming my eyes,
When savage Love
Jerked me up by the hair,
And threw me about,
And commanded me to stay up all night.
He said, "You are my slave,
The lover of a thousand girls.
Have you become so tough that you can lie here,
All alone and lonely?"
I jumped up barefoot and half dressed,
And ran off in all directions,
And got nowhere by any of them.
First I ran, and then I lingered,
And at last I was ashamed
To be wandering in the empty streets.
The voices of men,
The roar of traffic,
The songs of birds,
Even the barking of dogs,
Everything was still.
And me alone,
Afraid of my bed and sleep,
Ruled by a mighty lust.

PETRONIUS
(tr. Kenneth Rexroth)

That night will long delight us, Nealce,
That first cuddled you upon my breast,
The bed, and the image above it,
And the secret lamp by which you gave
Yourself, so softly, into my power.
For these, we can let age gain on us,
And enjoy the years which a little while
Will erase. It is fitting so
To prolong our love as we grow old,
And let what happened so suddenly,
Never suddenly stop.

PETRONIUS
(tr. Kenneth Rexroth)

Waking, my eyes, and in the night
My soul, seek you. Overcome
By my body, in my lonely bed,
I see you beside me, lying,
In the lying visions of sleep.
We would murder sleep
If you really came to me.

PETRONIUS
(tr. Kenneth Rexroth)

Hello. Hello. What's your name?
What's yours? You're too curious.
So are you. Have you got a date?
With anybody who likes me.
Do you want to go to dinner?
If you like. OK, how much?
You don't have to pay in advance.
That's odd. After you've slept with
Me, you can pay what you think
It's worth. Nothing wrong with that.
Where do you live, I'll call you.
Take it down. What time will you
Come? Whenever you say. Let's
Do it now. OK, walk ahead of me.

PHILODEMOS
(tr. Kenneth Rexroth)

In the middle of the night
I stole from my husband's bed
And came to you, soaked with rain.
And now, are we going to
Sit around, and not get down
To business, and not bill and coo,
And love like lovers ought to love?

PHILODEMOS
(tr. Kenneth Rexroth)

From Dante: La Vita Nuova

All ye that pass along Love's trodden way,
    Pause ye awhile and say
    If there be any grief like unto mine:
    I pray you that you hearken a short space
    Patiently, if my case
    Be not a piteous marvel and a sign.

Love (never, certes, for my worthless part,
    But of his own great heart,)
    Vouchsafed to me a life so calm and sweet
    That oft I heard folk question as I went
    What such great gladness meant:
    They spoke of it behind me in the street.

But now that fearless bearing is all gone
    Which with Love's hoarded wealth was given me;
    Till I am grown to be
    So poor that I have dread to think thereon.

And thus it is that I, being like as one
    Who is ashamed and hides his poverty,
    Without seem full of glee,
    And let my heart within travail and moan.

My lady carries love within her eyes;
    All that she looks on is made pleasanter;
    Upon her path men turn to gaze at her;
    He whom she greeteth feels his heart to rise,
And droops his troubled visage, full of sighs,
    And of his evil heart is then aware:
    Hate loves, and pride becomes a worshipper.
    O women, help to praise her in somewise.
Humbleness, and the hope that hopeth well,
    By speech of hers into the mind are brought,
    And who beholds is blessed oftenwhiles.
The look she hath when she a little smiles
    Cannot be said, nor holden in the thought;
    'Tis such a new and gracious miracle.

Beatrice is gone up into high Heaven,
    The kingdom where the angels are at peace;
    And lives with them; and to her friends is dead.
    Not by the frost of winter was she driven
    Away, like others; nor by summer-heats;
    But through a perfect gentleness, instead.
    For from the lamp of her meek lowlihead
    Such an exceeding glory went up hence
    That it woke wonder in the Eternal Sire,
    Until a sweet desire
    Enter'd Him for that lovely excellence,
    So that He bade her to Himself aspire:
    Counting this weary and most evil place
    Unworthy of a thing so full of grace.

(tr. Dante Gabriel Rosetti)

From Petrarch: Sonnets

Down my cheeks bitter tears incessant rain,
And my heart struggles with convulsive sighs,
When, Laura, upon you I turn my eyes,
For whom the world's allurements I disdain.
But when I see that gentle smile again,
That modest, sweet, and tender smile, arise,
It pours on every sense a blest surprise;
Lost in delight is all my torturing pain.
Too soon this heavenly transport sinks and dies:
When all thy soothing charms my fate removes
At thy departure from my ravished view.
To that sole refuge its firm faith approves
My spirit from my ravished bosom flies,
And winged with fond remembrance follows you.

(*tr. Capel Lofft*)

Some fowles there be, that haue so perfit sight
Against the sunne their eies for to defend:
And some, because the light doth them offend,
Neuer appeare, but in the darke, or night.
Other reioyce, to se the fire so bryght,
And wene to play in it, as they pretend:
But find contrary of it, that they intend.
Alas, of that sort may I be, by right.
For to withstand her loke I am not able:
Yet can I not hide me in no dark place:
So foloweth me remembrance of that face:
That with my teary eyn, swolne, and unstable,
My desteny to beholde her doth me lead:
And yet I knowe, I runne into the glead.

(*tr. Sir Thomas Wyatt*)

Alone and ever weary with dark care,
I seek the solitude of desert ways,
Casting about the while a timid gaze
Lest alien steps my refuge seek to share.
No other shield I find against the stare
Of curious folk; too clear my face displays
In ashen cheerlessness how cruel the blaze
That burns within, and lays my secret bare.
'Tis only hills, I think, and silent streams
And meadows and deep thickets that can know
The tenor of my life, from men concealed.
Yet not so wide I wander with my dreams
But Love comes with me, following where I go,
And long we parley on the lonely weald.

(tr. Thomas G. Bergin)

If I believed that death could make an end
To love's long torture that has laid me low,
My hand would long ere this have dealt the blow
To summon up oblivion, my friend.
But since I fear that I would but descend
From tears to tears, from woe to a worse woe,
On the gulf's edge, with half a step to go,
Irresolute, above the black I bend.
Oh, it were time the pitiless bow were drawn,
The cord pulled taut, aim taken carefully,
Time that the shaft into my heart were gone!
Thus I pray Love, and that deaf deity,
Death, whose pale colors I have not put on.
Why is she silent? She has forgotten me.

(tr. Morris Bishop)

O how unwary was I on that day,
When at the first Love smote me with his dart,
Till by degrees he triumphed o'er my heart,
And governed it with arbitrary sway!
I little thought its firmness would give way,
Its strength decrease by his insidious art:
So doth it fare with all who will depart
From safety's path, and amid dangers stray.
'Twere folly since resistance to pretend,
We now can only try if aught of prayer
Preferred by mortals Love will deign attend.
I ask not, for 'tis vain and claims no care,
That my fond passion should abate or end;
I ask that Laura may such passion share.

(tr. John Nott)

I've never wearied, love, of loving you,
Nor ever shall while living years endure,
But sharp self-hatred, sorrow without cure,
And tears that spring persistent,—these I rue.
So now the only boon my soul would sue
Is your name carven on my sepulture
Beneath whose marble weight my flesh secure
Could find, thus warranted, its rest anew.
Thus, if a living heart may please you still
Without your bruising it, oh then I pray
Be kind to mine; if such be not your will
And your disdain is still intent to slay
Or wound your lover then it chooses ill,
And, thankful, Love and I will go our way.

(tr. Thomas G. Bergin)

Oh, I shall always hate the window whence
Love, idle Love, transfixed me with his ray!
Why had it not sufficient force to slay?
It's good to die in life's young vehemence.
No, I must live, in lifelong penitence
Jailed on this earth. What, lifelong, did I say?
My pain will live when life has passed away;
The soul remembers how the heart laments.
Poor soul! You should have learned the lesson well:
In vain earth's mightiest do importune
Time to turn back its pages, or suspend
Its flight a moment. There's no more to tell.
Begone, sad soul! He cannot die too soon
Whose happy days have come to their last end.

(tr. Morris Bishop)

From Michelangelo

Remembrance of your eyes, O love, and hope
To find them kind at last (I am alive
Through them, and even blest),
Have found companions now in all the rest:
Reason, and will, and nature, all habits of me—
They all agree that to see *you* is best.
This is my life, indeed; should I change state,
I certainly would die,
Nor would I ever find pity at all
Far from your eyes (O God, how beautiful!).
Who has not seen these eyes is not born yet,
And if he ever should come to this earth
He would soon die: for not to fall
In love with these sweet eyes
Is not to live at all.

(tr. Joseph Tusiani)

Quick, run away from love, away from fire:
Harsh is the flame, and fatal the wound of the heart.
No use to reason or fight, once you start,
No use to find a place lower or higher.
Run, lovers, listen to me, I'm not a liar:
Strong is his arm, deadly and sharp his dart.
Oh learn from me your fatal imminent smart;
I warn you: he's the most merciless sire.

Quick, run away! At the first glance I thought
I would in time even come to terms with him:
But now my burn should tell you I did not.

(tr. Joseph Tusiani)

From Geoffrey Chaucer

MERCILES BEAUTE:
A TRIPLE ROUNDEL

Your yen two wol slee me sodenly,
I may the beaute of hem not sustene,
So woundeth hit through-out my herte kene.

And but your word wol helen hastily
My hertes wounde, whyl that hit is grene,
Your yen two wol slee me sodenly,
I may the beaute of hem not sustene.

Upon my trouthe I sey yow feithfully,
That ye ben of my lyf and deeth the quene;
For with my deeth the trouthe shal be sene.
Your yen two wol slee me sodenly,
I may the beaute of hem not sustene,
So woundeth hit through-out my herte kene.

CII: CANTUS TROILI

If no love is, O god, what fele I so?
And if love is, what thing and whiche is he?
If love be good, from whennes cometh my wo?
If it be wikke, a wonder thinketh me,
When every torment and adversitee
That cometh of him, may to me savory thinke;
For ay thurst I, the more that I it drinke.

And if that at myn owene lust I brenne,
Fro whennes cometh my wailing and my pleynte?
If harme agree me, wher-to pleyne I thenne?
I noot, ne why unwery that I feynte.
O quike deeth, o swete harm so queynte,
How may of thee in me swich quantitee,
But if that I consente that it be?

And if that I consente, I wrongfully
Compleyne, y-wis; thus possed to and fro,
Al sterelees with-inne a boot am I
A-mid the see, by-twixen windes two,
That in contrarie stonden ever-mo.
Allas! what is this wonder maladye?
For hete of cold, for cold of hete, I dye.

From William Shakespeare

UNDER THE GREENWOOD TREE

Amiens sings:

> Under the greenwood tree,
> Who loves to lie with me,
> And turn his merry note
> Unto the sweet bird's throat,
> Come hither, come hither, come hither:
> Here shall he see
> No enemy
> But winter and rough weather.
>
> Who doth ambition shun,
> And loves to live i' the sun,
> Seeking the food he eats,
> And pleased with what he gets,
> Come hither, come hither, come hither:
> Here shall he see
> No enemy
> But winter and rough weather.

Jacques replies:

> If it do come to pass
> That any man turn ass,
> Leaving his wealth and ease
> A stubborn will to please,
> Ducdame, ducdame, ducdame:
> Here shall he see
> Gross fools as he,
> An if he will come to me.

IT WAS A LOVER AND HIS LASS

It was a lover and his lass,
　With a hey, and a ho, and a hey nonino,
That o'er the green corn-field did pass,
　In the spring time, the only pretty ring time,
When birds do sing, hey ding a ding, ding;
Sweet lovers love the spring.

Between the acres of the rye,
　With a hey, and a ho, and a hey nonino,
These pretty country folks would lie,
　In the spring time, the only pretty ring time,
When birds do sing, hey ding a ding, ding;
Sweet lovers love the spring.

This carol they began that hour,
　With a hey, and a ho, and a hey nonino,
How that life was but a flower
　In the spring time, the only pretty ring time,
When birds do sing, hey ding a ding, ding;
Sweet lovers love the spring.

And, therefore, take the present time
　With a hey, and a ho, and a hey nonino,
For love is crowned with the prime
　In the spring time, the only pretty ring time,
When birds do sing, hey ding a ding, ding;
Sweet lovers love the spring.

SONNET XVIII

Shall I compare thee to a Summer's day?
Thou art more lovely and more temperate:
Rough winds do shake the darling buds of May,
And Summer's lease hath all too short a date:
Sometime too hot the eye of heaven shines,
And often is his gold complexion dimm'd;
And every fair from fair sometime declines,
By chance or nature's changing course untrimm'd:
But the eternal Summer shall not fade
Nor lose possession of that fair thou owest;
Nor shall Death brag thou wanderest in his shade,
When in eternal lines to time thou growest:
    So long as men can breathe, or eyes can see,
    So long lives this, and this gives life to thee.

SONNET XCVIII

From you have I been absent in the spring,
When proud-pied April, dress'd in all his trim,
Hath put a spirit of youth in everything,
That heavy Saturn laugh'd and leap'd with him.
Yet nor the lays of birds, nor the sweet smell
Of different flowers in odour and in hue,
Could make me any summer's story tell,
Or from their proud lap pluck them where they grew;
Nor did I wonder at the Lily's white,
Nor praise the deep vermilion in the Rose;
They were but sweet, but figures of delight,
Drawn after you, you pattern of all those.
   Yet seem'd it Winter still, and, you away,
    As with your shadow I with these did play.

SONNET CXXIX

Th' expense of Spirit in a waste of shame
Is lust in action; and till action, lust
Is perjured, murderous, bloody, full of blame,
Savage, extreme, rude, cruel, not to trust;
Enjoy'd no sooner but despised straight;
Past reason hunted; and, no sooner had,
Past reason hated, as a swallow'd bait
On purpose laid to make the taker mad:
Mad in pursuit, and in possession so;
Had, having, and in quest to have, extreme;
A bliss in proof, and proved, a very woe;
Before, a joy proposed; behind, a dream.
    All this the world well knows; yet none knows well
    To shun the heaven that leads men to this hell.

FROM ROMEO AND JULIET

Act I/Scene V

Romeo: O! she doth teach the torches to burn bright.
It seems she hangs upon the cheek of night
Like a rich jewel in an Ethiop's ear;
Beauty too rich for use, for earth too dear!
So shows a snowy dove trooping with crows,
As yonder lady o'er her fellows shows.
The measure done, I'll watch her place of stand,
And, touching hers, make blessed my rude hand.
Did my heart love till now? forswear it, sight!
For I ne'er saw true beauty till this night.

Act II/Scene II

Romeo: He jests at scars, that never felt a
    wound.
But, soft! what light through yonder window breaks?
It is the east, and Juliet is the sun!
Arise, fair sun, and kill the envious moon,
Who is already sick and pale with grief,
That thou her maid art far more fair than she:
Be not her maid, since she is envious;
Her vestal livery is but sick and green,
And none but fools do wear it; cast it off.
It is my lady; O! it is my love:
O! that she knew she were.
She speaks, yet she says nothing: what of that?
Her eye discourses; I will answer it.
I am too bold, 'tis not to me she speaks:
Two of the fairest stars in all the heaven,
Having some business, do entreat her eyes
To twinkle in their spheres till they return.
What if her eyes were there, they in her head?
The brightness of her cheek would shame those
    stars
As daylight doth a lamp; her eyes in heaven
Would through the airy region stream so bright

That birds would sing and think it were not
   night.
See! how she leans her cheek upon her hand:
O! that I were a glove upon that hand,
That I might touch that cheek.

Juliet: Ay me!

Romeo: She speaks:
O! speak again, bright angel; for thou art
As glorious to this night, being o'er my head,
As is a winged messenger of heaven
Unto the white-upturned wond'ring eyes
Of mortals, that fall back to gaze on him
When he bestrides the lazy-pacing clouds,
And sails upon the bosom of the air.

Juliet: O Romeo, Romeo! wherefore art thou
   Romeo?
Deny thy father, and refuse thy name;
Or, if thou wilt not, be but sworn my love,
And I'll no longer be a Capulet.

Romeo: Shall I hear more, or shall I
   speak at this?

Juliet: 'Tis but thy name that is my enemy;
Thou art thyself though, not a Montague.
What's Montague? it is nor hand, nor foot,
Nor arm, nor face, nor any other part
Belonging to a man. O! be some other name:
What's in a name? that which we call a rose
By any other name would smell as sweet;
So Romeo would, were he not Romeo call'd,
Retain that dear perfection which he owes
Without that title. Romeo, doff thy name;
And for that name, which is no part of thee,
Take all myself.

Romeo: I take thee at thy word.
Call me but love, and I'll be new baptiz'd;
Henceforth I never will be Romeo.

Juliet: What man art thou, that, thus bescreen'd
   in night,
So stumblest on my counsel?

Romeo: By a name
I know not how to tell thee who I am:

My name, dear saint, is hateful to myself,
Because it is an enemy to thee:
Had I it written, I would tear the word.

Juliet: My ears have not yet drunk a hundred
   words
   Of that tongue's uttering, yet I know the sound:
   Art thou not Romeo, and a Montague?

Romeo: Neither, fair maid, if either thee dislike.

Juliet: How cam'st thou hither, tell me, and
   wherefore?
   The orchard walls are high and hard to climb,
   And the place death, considering who thou art,
   If any of my kinsmen find thee here.

Romeo: With love's light wings did I o'er-perch
   these walls;
   For stony limits cannot hold love out,
   And what love can do that dares love attempt;
   Therefore thy kinsmen are no stop to me.

Juliet: If they do see thee they will murder thee.

Romeo: Alack! there lies more peril in thine eye
   Than twenty of their swords: look thou but
   sweet,
   And I am proof against their enmity.

Juliet: I would not for the world they saw thee here.

Romeo: I have night's cloak to hide me from
   their eyes;
   And but thou love me, let them find me here;
   My life were better ended by their hate,
   Than death prorogued, wanting of thy love.

Juliet: By whose direction found'st thou out
   this place?

Romeo: By Love, that first did prompt me to
   inquire;
   He lent me counsel, and I lent him eyes.
   I am no pilot; yet, wert thou as far
   As that vast shore wash'd with the furthest sea,
   I would adventure for such merchandise.

Juliet: Thou know'st the mask of night is on
   my face,

Else would a maiden blush bepaint my cheek
For that which thou hast heard me speak tonight.
Fain would I dwell on form, fain, fain deny
What I have spoke: but farewell compliment!
Dost thou love me? I know thou wilt say 'Ay,'
And I will take thy word; yet, if thou swear'st,
Thou mayst prove false; at lovers' perjuries,
They say, Jove laughs. O gentle Romeo!
If thou dost love, pronounce it faithfully:
Or if thou think'st I am too quickly won,
I'll frown and be perverse and say thee nay,
So thou wilt woo; but else, not for the world.
In truth, fair Montague, I am too fond,
And therefore thou mayst think my behaviour
    light:
But trust me, gentleman I'll prove more true
Than those that have more cunning to be
    strange.
I should have been more strange, I must confess,
But that thou over-heard'st, ere I was 'ware,
My true love's passion: therefore pardon me,
And not impute this yielding to light love,
Which the dark night hath so discovered.

Romeo: Lady, by yonder blessed moon I swear
    That tips with silver all these fruit-tree tops,—

Juliet: O! swear not by the moon, the incon-
    stant moon,
    That monthly changes in her circled orb,
    Lest that thy love prove likewise variable.

Romeo: What shall I swear by?

Juliet: Do not swear at all;
    Or, if thou wilt, swear by thy gracious self,
    Which is the god of my idolatry.
    And I'll believe thee.

Romeo: If my heart's dear love—

Juliet: Well, do not swear. Although I joy in
    thee,
    I have no joy of this contract to-night:
    It is too rash, too unadvis'd, too sudden;
    Too like the lightning, which doth cease to be
    Ere one can say it lightens. Sweet, good-night!

This bud of love, by summer's ripening breath,
May prove a beauteous flower when next we
meet.
Good-night, good-night! as sweet repose and
rest
Come to thy heart as that within my breast!

Romeo: O! wilt thou leave me so unsatisfied?

Juliet: What satisfaction canst thou have to-
night?

Romeo: The exchange of thy love's faithful vow
for mine.

Juliet: I gave thee mine before thou didst re-
quest it;
And yet I would it were to give again.

Romeo: Wouldst thou withdraw it? for what
purpose, love?

Juliet: But to be frank, and give it thee again.
And yet I wish but for the thing I have:
My bounty is as boundless as the sea,
My love as deep; the more I give to thee,
The more I have, for both are infinite.
I hear some noise within; dear love, adieu!
Anon, good nurse! Sweet Montague, be true.
Stay but a little, I will come again.

Romeo: O blessed, blessed night! I am afeared,
Being in night, all this is but a dream,
Too flattering-sweet to be substantial.

Juliet: Three words, dear Romeo, and good-
night indeed.
If that thy bent of love be honourable,
Thy purpose marriage, send me word to-
morrow,
By one that I'll procure to come to thee,
Where, and what time, thou wilt perform the rite;
And all my fortunes at thy foot I'll lay,
And follow thee my lord throughout the world.

Nurse: Madam!

Juliet: I come, anon.—But if thou mean'st not
well,

I do beseech thee,—

Nurse: Madam!

Juliet: By and by; I come:—
   To cease thy suit, and leave me to my grief:
   To-morrow will I send.

Romeo: So thrive my soul,—

Juliet: A thousand times good-night!

Romeo: A thousand times the worse, to want
      thy light.
   Love goes toward love, as schoolboys from
      their books;
   But love from love, toward school with heavy
      looks.

Juliet: Hist! Romeo, hist! O! for a falconer's
      voice,
   To lure this tassel-gentle back again.
   Bondage is hoarse, and may not speak aloud,
   Else would I tear the cave where Echo lies,
   And make her airy tongue more hoarse than
      mine,
   With repetition of my Romeo's name.

Romeo: It is my soul that calls upon my name:
   How silver-sweet sound lovers' tongues by
      night,
   Like softest music to attending ears!

Juliet: Romeo!

Romeo: My dear!

Juliet: At what o'clock to-morrow
   Shall I send to thee?

Romeo: At the hour of nine.

Juliet: I will not fail; 'tis twenty years till then.
   I have forgot why I did call thee back.

Romeo: Let me stand here till thou remember it.

Juliet: I shall forget, to have thee still stand
      there,
   Remembering how I love thy company.

Romeo: And I'll still stay, to have thee still
    forget,
  Forgetting any other home but this.

Juliet: 'Tis almost morning; I would have thee
    gone;
  And yet no further than a wanton's bird,
  Who lets it hop a little from her hand,
  Like a poor prisoner in his twisted gyves,
  And with a silk thread plucks it back again,
  So loving-jealous of his liberty.

Romeo: I would I were thy bird.

Juliet: Sweet, so would I:
  Yet I should kill thee with much cherishing.
  Good-night, good-night! parting is such sweet
    sorrow
  That I shall say good-night till it be morrow.

Romeo: Sleep dwell upon thine eyes, peace in
    thy breast!
  Would I were sleep and peace, so sweet to rest!
  Hence will I to my ghostly father's cell,
  His help to crave, and my dear hap to tell.

Act III/Scene II

Juliet: Gallop apace, you fiery-footed steeds,
  Towards Phoebus' lodging; such a waggoner
  As Phaethon would whip you to the west,
  And bring in cloudy night immediately.
  Spread thy close curtain, love-performing night!
  That runaway's eyes may wink, and Romeo
  Leap to these arms, untalk'd of and unseen!
  Lovers can see to do their amorous rites
  By their own beauties; or, if love be blind,
  It best agrees with night. Come, civil night,
  Thou sober-suited matron, all in black,
  And learn me how to lose a winning match,
  Play'd for a pair of stainless maidenhoods:
  Hood my unmann'd blood, bating in my cheeks,
  With thy black mantle; till strange love, grown
    bold,
  Think true love acted simple modesty.

Come, night! come, Romeo! come, thou day in
   night!
For thou wilt lie upon the wings of night,
Whiter than new snow on a raven's back.
Come, gentle night; come, loving, black-brow'd
   night,
Give me my Romeo: and, when he shall die,
Take him and cut him out in little stars,
And he will make the face of heaven so fine
That all the world will be in love with night,
And pay no worship to the garish sun.
O! I have bought the mansion of a love,
But not possess'd it, and, though I am sold,
Not yet enjoy'd. So tedious is this day
As is the night before some festival
To an impatient child that hath new robes
And may not wear them. O! here comes my
   nurse,
And she brings news; and every tongue that
   speaks
But Romeo's name speaks heavenly eloquence.

VIXI PUELLIS NUPER IDONEUS . . .

They flee from me that sometime did me seek,
　　　　With naked foot stalking in my chamber:
I have seen them gentle, tame, and meek,
　　That now are wild, and do not once remember
　　That sometime they have put themselves in danger
To take bread at my hand; and now they range,
Busily seeking with a continual change.
Thanked be fortune, it hath been otherwise
　　Twenty times better; but once, in special,
In thin array, after a pleasant guise,
　　When her loose gown from her shoulders did fall,
　　And she me caught in her arms long and small,
Therewith all sweetly did me kiss,
And softly said, 'Dear heart, how like you this?'
It was no dream; I lay broad waking:
　　But all is turned, thorough my gentleness,
Into a strange fashion of forsaking;
　　And I have leave to go, of her goodness;
　　And she also to use new-fangleness.
But since that I unkindely so am served,
'How like you this?'—what hath she now deserved?

Sir Thomas Wyatt

LOVE IS A SICKNESS

Love is a sickness full of woes,
  All remedies refusing;
A plant that with most cutting grows,
  Most barren with best using.
    Why so?
More we enjoy it, more it dies;
If not enjoy'd, it sighing cries—
    Heigh ho!

Love is a torment of the mind,
  A tempest everlasting;
And Jove hath made it of a kind
  Not well, nor full nor fasting.
    Why so?
More we enjoy it, more it dies;
If not enjoy'd, it sighing cries—
    Heigh ho!

SAMUEL DANIEL

THE PARTING

Since there's no help, come let us kiss and part—
Nay, I have done, you get no more of me;
And I am glad, yea, glad with all my heart,
That thus so cleanly I myself can free.
Shake hands for ever, cancel all our vows,
And when we meet at any time again,
Be it not seen in either of our brows
That we one jot of former love retain.
Now at the last gasp of Love's latest breath,
When, his pulse failing, Passion speechless lies,
When Faith is kneeling by his bed of death,
And Innocence is closing up his eyes,
   —Now if thou wouldst, when all have given him over,
   From death to life thou might'st him yet recover.

MICHAEL DRAYTON

THE PASSIONATE SHEPHERD TO HIS LOVE

Come live with me and be my Love,
And we will all the pleasures prove
That hills and valleys, dales and fields,
Or woods or steep mountain yields.

And we will sit upon the rocks,
And see the shepherds feed their flocks
By shallow rivers, to whose falls
Melodious birds sing madrigals.

And I will make thee beds of roses
And a thousand fragrant posies;
A cap of flowers, and a kirtle
Embroider'd all with leaves of myrtle.

A gown made of the finest wool
Which from our pretty lambs we pull;
Fair-lined slippers for the cold,
With buckles of the purest gold.

A belt of straw and ivy-buds
With coral clasps and amber studs:
And if these pleasures may thee move,
Come live with me and be my Love.

CHRISTOPHER MARLOWE

DEVOTION (ii)

Follow your saint, follow with accents sweet!
Haste you, sad notes, fall at her flying feet!
There, wrapt in cloud of sorrow, pity move,
And tell the ravisher of my soul I perish for her love:
But if she scorns my never-ceasing pain,
Then burst with sighing in her sight, and ne'er return again!

All that I sung still to her praise did tend;
Still she was first, still she my songs did end;
Yet she my love and music both doth fly,
The music that her echo is and beauty's sympathy:
Then let my notes pursue her scornful flight!
It shall suffice that they were breathed and died for her delight.

THOMAS CAMPION

TO CELIA

Drink to me only with thine eyes,
And I will pledge with mine;
Or leave a kiss but in the cup
And I'll not look for wine.
The thirst that from the soul doth rise
Doth ask a drink divine;
But might I of Jove's nectar sup,
I would not change for thine.

I sent thee late a rosy wreath,
Not so much honouring thee
As giving it a hope that there
It could not wither'd be;
But thou thereon didst only breathe,
And sent'st it back to me;
Since when it grows, and smells, I swear,
Not of itself but thee!

BEN JONSON

SIMPLEX MUNDITIIS

Still to be neat, still to be drest,
As you were going to a feast;
Still to be powder'd, still perfumed:
Lady, it is to be presumed,
Though art's hid causes are not found,
All is not sweet, all is not sound.

Give me a look, give me a face
That makes simplicity a grace;
Robes loosely flowing, hair as free:
Such sweet neglect more taketh me
Than all th' adulteries of art;
They strike mine eyes, but not my heart.

BEN JONSON

THE POET LOVES A MISTRESS BUT NOT TO MARRY

I do not love to wed,
Though I do like to woo;
And for a maidenhead
I'll beg and buy it too.

I'll praise and I'll approve
Those maids that never vary;
And fervently I'll love
But yet I would not marry.

I'll hug, I'll kiss, I'll play,
And, cock-like, hens I'll tread,
And sport in any way
But in the bridal bed.

For why? that man is poor
Who hath but one of many,
But crown'd he is with store
That, single, may have many.

Why, then, say what is he,
To freedom so unknown,
Who, having two or three,
Will be content with one?

ROBERT HERRICK

TO THE VIRGINS, TO MAKE MUCH OF TIME

Gather ye rosebuds while ye may,
  Old Time is still a-flying:
And this same flower that smiles to-day
  To-morrow will be dying.

The glorious lamp of heaven, the sun,
  The higher he's a-getting,
The sooner will his race be run,
  And nearer he's to setting.

That age is best which is the first,
  When youth and blood are warmer;
But being spent, the worse, and worst
  Times still succeed the former.

Then be not coy, but use your time,
  And while ye may, go marry:
For having lost but once your prime,
  You may for ever tarry.

ROBERT HERRICK

ON A GIRDLE

That which her slender waist confined
Shall now my joyful temples bind;
No monarch but would give his crown
His arms might do what this has done.

It was my Heaven's extremest sphere,
The pale which held that lovely deer:
My joy, my grief, my hope, my love,
Did all within this circle move.

A narrow compass! and yet there
Dwelt all that's good, and all that's fair!
Give me but what this ribband bound,
Take all the rest the sun goes round!

EDMUND WALLER

GO, LOVELY ROSE

Go, lovely Rose—
   Tell her that wastes her time and me,
   That now she knows,
When I resemble her to thee,
How sweet and fair she seems to be.

   Tell her that's young,
And shuns to have her graces spied,
   That hadst thou sprung
In deserts where no men abide,
Thou must have uncommended died.

   Small is the worth
Of beauty from the light retired:
   Bid her come forth,
Suffer herself to be desired,
And not blush so to be admired.

   Then die—that she
The common fate of all things rare
   May read in thee;
How small a part of time they share
That are so wondrous sweet and fair!

EDMUND WALLER

THE CONSTANT LOVER

Out upon it, I have loved
   Three whole days together!
And am like to love three more,
   If it prove fair weather.

Time shall moult away his wings
   Ere he shall discover
In the whole wide world again
   Such a constant lover.

But the spite on 't is, no praise
   Is due at all to me:
Love with me had made no stays,
   Had it any been but she.

Had it any been but she,
   And that very face,
There had been at least ere this
   A dozen dozen in her place.

SIR JOHN SUCKLING

WHY SO PALE AND WAN?

Why so pale and wan, fond lover?
   Prithee, why so pale?
Will, when looking well can't move her,
   Looking ill prevail?
   Prithee, why so pale?

Why so dull and mute, young sinner?
   Prithee, why so mute?
Will, when speaking well can't win her,
   Saying nothing do 't?
   Prithee, why so mute?

Quit, quit for shame! This will not move;
   This cannot take her.
If of herself she will not love,
   Nothing can make her:
   The devil take her!

SIR JOHN SUCKLING

TO HIS COY MISTRESS

Had we but world enough, and time,
This coyness, Lady, were no crime.
We would sit down and think which way
To walk and pass our long love's day.
Thou by the Indian Ganges' side
Shouldst rubies find: I by the tide
Of Humber would complain. I would
Love you ten years before the Flood,
And you should, if you please, refuse
Till the conversion of the Jews.
My vegetable love should grow
Vaster than empires, and more slow;
An hundred years should go to praise
Thine eyes and on thy forehead gaze;
Two hundred to adore each breast;
But thirty thousand to the rest;
An age at least to every part,
And the last age should show your heart;
For, Lady, you deserve this state,
Nor would I love at lower rate.
   But at my back I always hear
Time's winged chariot hurrying near;
And yonder all before us lie
Deserts of vast eternity.
Thy beauty shall no more be found,
Nor, in thy marble vault, shall sound
My echoing song: then worms shall try
That long preserved virginity,
And your quaint honour turn to dust,
And into ashes all my lust:
The grave's a fine and private place,
But none, I think, do there embrace.
   Now therefore, while the youthful hue
Sits on thy skin like morning dew,
And while thy willing soul transpires
At every pore with instant fires,
Now let us sport us while we may,
And now, like amorous birds of prey,
Rather at once our time devour
Than languish in his slow-chapt power.
Let us roll all our strength and all
Our sweetness up into one ball,

And tear our pleasures with rough strife
Thorough the iron gates of life:
Thus, though we cannot make our sun
Stand still, yet we will make him run.

Andrew Marvell

TO HIS MISTRESS GOING TO BED

Come, madam, come, all rest my powers defy;
Until I labour, I in labour lie.
The foe ofttimes, having the foe in sight,
Is tired with standing, though he never fight.
Off with that girdle, like heaven's zone glittering,
But a far fairer world encompassing.
Unpin that spangled breast-plate, which you wear,
That th' eyes of busy fools may be stopp'd there.
Unlace yourself, for that harmonious chime
Tells me from you that now it is bed-time.
Off with that happy busk, which I envy,
That still can be, and still can stand so nigh.
Your gown going off such beauteous state reveals,
As when from flowery meads th' hill's shadow steals.
Off with your wiry coronet, and show
The hairy diadems which on you do grow.
Off with your hose and shoes; then softly tread
In this love's hallow'd temple, this soft bed.
In such white robes heaven's angels used to be
Revealed to men; thou, angel, bring'st with thee
A heaven-like Mahomet's paradise; and though
Ill spirits walk in white, we easily know
By this these angels from an evil sprite;
Those set our hairs, but these our flesh upright.
    License my roving hands, and let them go
Before, behind, between, above, below.
Oh, my America, my Newfoundland,
My kingdom, safest when the one man mann'd,
My mine of precious stones, my empery;
How am I blest in thus discovering thee!
To enter in these bonds, is to be free;
Then where my hand is set, my soul shall be.
    Full nakedness! All joys are due to thee;
As souls embodied, bodies unclothed must be
To taste whole joys. Gems which you women use
Are like Atlanta's ball cast in men's views;
That, when a fool's eye lighteth on a gem,
His earthly soul might court that, not them.
Like pictures, or like books' gay coverings made
For laymen, are all women thus array'd.
Themselves are only mystic books, which we
—Whom their imputed grace will dignify—
Must see reveal'd. Then, since that I may know,

As liberally as to thy midwife show
Thyself; cast all, yea, this white linen hence;
There is no penance due to innocence:
To teach thee, I am naked first; why then,
What needst thou have more covering than a man?

JOHN DONNE

THE CANONIZATION

For Godsake hold your tongue, and let me love,
  Or chide my palsie, or my gout,
My five gray haires, or ruin'd fortune flout,
    With wealth your state, your minde with Arts improve,
      Take you a course, get you a place,
      Observe his honour, or his grace,
Or the Kings reall, or his stamped face
    Contemplate, what you will, approve,
    So you will let me love.

Alas, alas, who's injur'd by my love?
  What merchants ships have my sighs drown'd?
Who saies my teares have overflow'd his ground?
    When did my colds a forward spring remove?
      When did the heats which my veines fill
      Adde one more to the plaguie Bill?
Soldiers finde warres, and Lawyers finde out still
    Litigious men, which quarrels move,
    Though she and I do love.

Call us what you will, wee are made such by love;
  Call her one, mee another flye,
We'are Tapers too, and at our owne cost die,
    And wee in us finde the'Eagle and the Dove.
      The Phoenix riddle hath more wit
      By us, we two being one, are it.
So to one neutrall thing both sexes fit,
    Wee dye and rise the same, and prove
    Mysterious by this love.

Wee can dye bye it, if not live by love,
  And if unfit for tombes and hearse
Our legend bee, it will be fit for verse;
    And if no peece of Chronicle wee prove,
      We'll build in sonnets pretty roomes;
      As well a well wrought urne becomes
The greatest ashes, as halfe-acre tombes,
    And by these hymnes, all shall approve
    Us *Canoniz'd* for Love:

And thus invoke us; You whom reverend love
  Made one anothers hermitage;
You, to whom love was peace, that now is rage;

Who did the whole worlds soule contract, and drove
   Into the glasses of your eyes
   So made such mirrors, and such spies,
Countries, Townes, Courts: Beg from above
A patterne of your love!

JOHN DONNE

A SHEPHERD KEPT SHEEP ON A
HILL SO HIGH

A Shepherd kept Sheep on a Hill so high,
And there came a pretty Maid passing by,
Shepherd, quoth she, dost thou want e'er a Wife,
No by my troth I'm not weary of my Life.

Shepherd for thee I care not a Fly,
For thou'st not the Face with a fair Maid to lie,
How now my Damsel, say'st thou me so,
Thou shalt taste of my bottle before thou dost go.

Then he took her and laid her upon the Ground,
And made her believe that the World went round,
Look yonder my Shepherd, look yonder I spy
There are fine pretty Babies that dance in the Sky.

And now they are vanisht, and now they appear,
Sure they will tell Stories of what we do here,
Lie still my dear Chloris, enjoy thy Conceit,
For the Babes are too young and too little to prate.

See how the Heavens fly swifter than Day,
Rise quickly, or they will all run away,
Rise quickly my Shepherd, quickly I tell ye,
For the Sun, Moon and Stars are got all in my Belly.

O dear, where am I? pray shew me the way,
Unto my Father's House hard by,
If he chance to Chide me for staying so long,
I'll tell him the fumes of your Bottle were strong.

And now thou hast brought my Body to shame,
I prithee now tell me what is thy Name,
Why Robin in the Rushes my Name is, quoth he,
But I think I told her quite contrary.

Then for Robin in the Rushes, she did enquire,
But he hung down his Head, and he would not come nigh
  her,
He wink'd with one Eye, as if he had been Blind,
And he drew one Leg after a great way behind.

                                    THOMAS D'URFEY

PHRYNE

Phryne had talents for mankind;
Open she was and unconfin'd,
   Like some free port of trade:
Merchants unloaded here their freight,
And agents from each foreign state
   Here first their entry made.

Her learning and good breeding such,
Whether th' Italian or the Dutch;
   Spaniards or French, came to her,
To all obliging she'd appear;
'T was Si Signior, 't was Yaw Mynheer,
   'T was S'il vous plait, Monsieur.

Obscure by birth, renown'd by crimes,
Still changing names, religions, climes,
   At length she turns a bride;
In diamonds, pearls, and rich brocades,
She shines the first of batter'd jades,
   And flutters in her pride.

So have I known those insects fair
(Which curious Germans hold so rare)
   Still vary shapes and dyes;
Still gain new titles with new forms;
First grubs obscene, then wriggling worms,
   Then painted butterflies.

ALEXANDER POPE

JENNY KISS'D ME

Jenny kiss'd me when we met,
   Jumping from the chair she sat in;
Time, you thief, who love to get
   Sweets into your list, put that in!
Say I'm weary, say I'm sad,
   Say that health and wealth have miss'd me,
Say I'm growing old, but add,
   Jenny kiss'd me.

LEIGH HUNT

From Robert Burns

ODE TO SPRING

When maukin bucks, at early fucks,
    In dewy glens are seen, Sir;
And birds, on boughs, take off their mows,
    Amang the leaves sae green, Sir;
Latona's sun looks liquorish on
    Dame Nature's grand impetus,
Till his prick go rise, then westward flies
    To roger Madame Thetis.

Yon wandering rill that marks the hill,
    And Glances o'er the brae, Sir,
Slides by a bower where many a flower
    Sheds fragrance on the day, Sir;
There Damon lay, with Sylvia gay,
    To love they thought no crime, Sir;
The wild-birds sang, the echoes rang,
    While Damon's arse beat time, Sir.

First, wi' the thrust, his thrust and push
    Had compass large and long, Sir;
The blackbird next, his tuneful text,
    Was bolder, clear and strong, Sir;
The linnet's lay came then in play,
    And the lark that soar'd aboon, Sir;
Till Damon, fierce, mistim'd his arse,
    And fuck'd quite out o' tune, Sir.

NINE INCH WILL PLEASE A LADY

Come rede me, dame, come tell me, dame,
   My dame, come tell me truly,
What length o' graith, when weel ca'd hame
   Will ser'e a woman duly?
The carlin clew her wanton tail,
   Her wanton tail sae ready;
I learnt a sang in Annandale,
   Nine inch will please a lady.

But for a countrie cunt like mine,
   In sooth we're nae sae gentle;
We'll take twa thumb-bread to the nine,
   And that's a sonsie pintle.
O leeze me on my Charlie lad!
   I'll ne'er forget my Charlie;
Twa roarin handfu' and a daud,
   He nidg't it in fu' rarely.

But weary fa' the laithern doup,
   And may it ne'er ken thrivin';
It's no the length that gars me loup,
   But it's the double drivin'.
Come nidge me Tam, come nodge me Tam,
   Come nidge me o'er the nyvel;
Come loose and lug your batterin' ram,
   And thrash him at my gyvel.

GREEN GROW THE RASHES

Green grow the rashes, O,
  Green grow the rashes, O;
The sweetest bed that e'er I got,
  Was the bellies o' the lasses, O!

'Twas late yestreen I met wi' ane
  And vow but she was gentle, O;
Ae hand she put to my gravat
  The tither to my pintle, O.

I dought na speak, yet was na fly'd,
  My heart play'd duntie, duntie, O,
A' ceremonie laid aside,
  I fairly found her cuntie, O.

The down-bed, the feather-bed,
  The bed amang the rashes-O;
Yet a' the beds is nae sae saft
  As the bellies o' the lasses-O!

Green grow the rashes, O,
  Green grow the rashes, O;
The lasses they hae wimble bores,
  The widows they hae gashes, O!

THE INDIAN SERENADE

I arise from dreams of thee
   In the first sweet sleep of night,
When the winds are breathing low,
   And the stars are shining bright.
I arise from dreams of thee,
   And a spirit in my feet
Hath led me—who knows how?
   To thy chamber window, Sweet!

The wandering airs they faint
   On the dark, the silent stream—
And the Champak's odours (pine)
   Like sweet thoughts in a dream;
The nightingale's complaint,
   It dies upon her heart,
As I must on thine,
   O beloved as thou art!

O lift me from the grass!
   I die! I faint! I fail!
Let thy love in kisses rain
   On my lips and eyelids pale.
My cheek is cold and white, alas!
   My heart beats loud and fast:
O press it to thine own again,
   Where it will break at last!

PERCY BYSSHE SHELLEY

LA BELLE DAME SANS MERCI

'O what can ail thee, knight-at-arms,
    Alone and palely loitering?
The sedge is wither'd from the lake,
    And no birds sing.

'O what can ail thee, knight-at-arms,
    So haggard and so woe-begone?
The squirrel's granary is full,
    And the harvest's done.

'I see a lily on thy brow
    With anguish moist and fever dew;
And on thy cheek a fading rose
    Fast withereth too.

'I met a lady in the meads,
    Full beautiful—a faery's child,
Her hair was long, her foot was light,
    And her eyes were wild.

'I made a garland for her head,
    And bracelets too, and fragrant zone;
She look'd at me as she did love,
    And made sweet moan.

'I set her on my pacing steed
    And nothing else saw all day long,
For sideways would she lean, and sing
    A faery's song.

'She found me roots of relish sweet,
    And honey wild and manna dew,
And sure in language strange she said,
    "I love thee true!"

'She took me to her elfin grot,
    And there she wept and sigh'd full sore;
And there I shut her wild, wild eyes
    With kisses four.

'And there she lulled me asleep,
 And there I dream'd—Ah! woe betide!
The lastest dream I ever dream'd
 On the cold hill's side.

'I saw pale kings and princes too,
 Pale warriors, death-pale were they all;
Who cried—"La belle Dame sans Merci
 Hath thee in thrall!"

'I saw their starved lips in the gloam
 With horrid warning gaped wide,
And I awoke and found me here
 On the cold hill's side.

'And this is why I sojourn here
 Alone and palely loitering,
Though the sedge is wither'd from the lake,
 And no birds sing.'

JOHN KEATS

WHERE BE YOU GOING, YOU DEVON MAID?

Where be you going, you Devon maid?
  And what have ye there in the basket?
Ye tight little fairy, just fresh from the dairy,
  Will ye give me some cream if I ask it?

I love your hills and I love your dales,
  And I love your flocks a-bleating;
But oh, on the heather to lie together,
  With both our hearts a-beating!

I'll put your basket all safe in a nook;
  Your shawl I'll hang on a willow;
And we will sigh in the daisy's eye,
  And kiss on a grass-green pillow.

JOHN KEATS

VITAE SUMMA BREVIS SPEM NOS VETAT
INCOHARE LONGAM

They are not long, the weeping and the laughter,
  Love and desire and hate:
I think they have no portion in us after
    We pass the gate.

They are not long, the days of wine and roses:
  Out of a misty dream
Our path emerges for a while, then closes
    Within a dream.

ERNEST DOWSON

LOVE ON THE FARM

What large, dark hands are those at the window
Grasping in the golden light
Which weaves its way through the evening wind
    At my heart's delight?

Ah, only the leaves! But in the west
I see a redness suddenly come
Into the evening's anxious breast—
    'Tis the wound of love goes home!

The woodbine creeps abroad
Calling low to her lover:
    The sun-lit flirt who all the day
    Has poised above her lips in play
    And stolen kisses, shallow and gay
    Of pollen, now has gone away—
        She woos the mother with her sweet, low word;
And when above her his moth-wings hover
Then her bright breast she will uncover
And yield her honey-drop to her lover.

Into the yellow, evening glow
Saunters a man from the farm below;
Leans, and looks in at the low-built shed
Where the swallow has hung her marriage bed.

    The bird lies warm against the wall.
    She glances quick her startled eyes
    Towards him, then she turns away
    Her small head, making warm display
    Of red upon her throat. Her terrors sway
    Her out of the nest's warm busy ball,
    Whose plaintive cry is heard as she flies
    In one blue stoop from out the sties
    into the twilight's empty hall.

Oh, water-hen, beside the rushes,
Hide your quaintly scarlet blushes,
Still your quick tail, lie still as dead,
Till the distance folds over his ominous tread!

The rabbit presses back her ears,
Turns back her liquid, anguished eyes
And crouches low; then with wild spring
Spurts from the terror of his oncoming;
To be choked back, the wire ring
Her frantic efforts throttling:
   Piteous brown ball of quivering fears!
Ah, soon in his large, hard hands she dies,
And swings all loose from the swing of his walk!
Yet calm and kindly are his eyes
And ready to open in brown surprise
Should I not answer to his talk
Or should he my tears surmise.

I hear his hand on the latch, and rise from my chair
Watching the door open; he flashes bare
His strong teeth in a smile, and flashes his eyes
In a smile like triumph upon me; then careless-wise
He flings the rabbit soft on the table board
And comes towards me: he! the uplifted sword
Of his hand against my bosom! and oh, the broad
Blade of his glance that asks me to applaud
His coming! With his hand he turns my face to him
And caresses me with his fingers that still smell grim
Of rabbit's fur! God, I am caught in a snare!
I know not what fine wire is round my throat;
I only know I let him finger there
My pulse of life, and let him nose like a stoat
Who sniffs with joy before he drinks the blood.

And down his mouth comes to my mouth! and down
His bright dark eyes come over me, like a hood
Upon my mind! his lips meet mine, and a flood
Of sweet fire sweeps across me, so I drown
Against him, die, and find death good.

D. H. LAWRENCE

REPROACH

Had I but known yesterday,
Helen, you could discharge the ache
    out of the cloud;
Had I known yesterday you could take
The turgid electric ache away,
   Drink it up with your proud
White body, as lovely white lightning
Is drunk from an agonised sky by the earth,
I might have hated you, Helen.

But since my limbs gushed full of fire,
Since from out of my blood and bone
    Poured a heavy flame
To you, earth of my atmosphere, stone
Of my steel, lovely white flint of desire,
    You have no name.
Earth of my swaying atmosphere,
Substance of my inconstant breath,
I cannot but cleave to you.

Since you have drunken up the drear
Painful electric storm, and death
    Is washed from the blue
Of my eyes, I see you beautiful.
You are strong and passive and beautiful,
I come like winds that uncertain hover;
    But you
Are the earth I hover over.

D. H. LAWRENCE

LEDA AND THE SWAN

A sudden blow: the great wings beating still
Above the staggering girl, her thighs caressed
By the dark webs, her nape caught in his bill,
He holds her helpless breast upon his breast.

How can those terrified vague fingers push
The feathered glory from her loosening thighs?
And how can body, laid in that white rush,
But feel the strange heart beating where it lies?

A shudder in the loins engenders there
The broken wall, the burning roof and tower
And Agamemnon dead.

          Being so caught up,
So mastered by the brute blood of the air,
Did she put on his knowledge with his power
Before the indifferent beak could let her drop?

WILLIAM BUTLER YEATS

LAMENT

When I was a windy boy and a bit
And the black spit of the chapel fold,
(Sighed the old ram rod, dying of women),
I tiptoed shy in the gooseberry wood,
The rude owl cried like a telltale tit,
I skipped in a blush as the big girls rolled
Ninepin down on the donkey's common,
And on seesaw sunday nights I wooed
Whoever I would with my wicked eyes,
The whole of the moon I could love and leave
All the green leaved little weddings' wives
In the coal black bush and let them grieve.

When I was a gusty man and a half
And the black beast of the beetles' pews,
(Sighed the old ram rod, dying of bitches),
Not a boy and a bit in the wick—
Dipping moon and drunk as a new dropped calf,
I whistled all night in the twisted flues,
Midwives grew in the midnight ditches,
And the sizzling beds of the town cried, Quick!—
Whenever I dove in a breast high shoal,
Wherever I ramped in the clover quilts,
Whatsoever I did in the coal-
Black night, I left my fiery prints.

When I was a man you could call a man
And the black cross of the holy house,
(Sighed the old ram rod, dying of welcome),
Brandy and ripe in my bright, bass prime,
No springtailed tom in the red hot town
With every simmering woman his mouse
But a hillocky bull in the swelter

Of summer come in his great good time
To the sultry, biding herds, I said,
Oh, time enough when the blood creeps cold,
And I lie down but to sleep in bed,
For my sulking, skulking, coal black soul!

When I was a half of the man I was
And serve me right as the preachers warn,
(Sighed the old ram rod, dying of downfall),
No flailing calf or cat in a flame
Or hickory bull in milky grass
But a black sheep with a crumpled horn,
At last the soul from its foul mousehole
Slunk pouting out when the limp time came;
And I gave my soul a blind, slashed eye,
Gristle and rind, and a roarer's life,
And I shoved it into the coal black sky
To find a woman's soul for a wife.

Now I am a man no more no more
And a black reward for a roaring life,
(Sighed the old ram rod, dying of strangers),
Tidy and cursed in my dove cooed room
I lie down thin and hear the good bells jaw—
For, oh, my soul found a sunday wife
In the coal black sky and she bore angels!
Harpies around me out of her womb!
Chastity prays for me, piety sings,
Innocence blesses my last black breath,
Modesty swaddles my thighs with her wings,
And all the deadly virtues plague my death!

DYLAN THOMAS

LATE-FLOWERING LUST

My head is bald, my breath is bad,
    Unshaven is my chin,
I have not now the joys I had
    When I was young in sin.

I run my fingers down your dress
    With brandy-certain aim
And you respond to my caress
    And maybe feel the same.

But I've a picture of my own
    On this reunion night,
Wherein two skeletons are shewn
    To hold each other tight;

Dark sockets look on emptiness
    Which once was loving-eyed,
The mouth that opens for a kiss
    Has got no tongue inside.

I cling to you inflamed with fear
    As now you cling to me,
I feel how frail you are my dear
    And wonder what will be—

A week? or twenty years remain?
    And then—what kind of death?
A losing fight with frightful pain
    Or gasping fight for breath?

Too long we let our bodies cling,
    We cannot hide disgust
At all the thoughts that in us spring
    From this late-flowering lust.

JOHN BETJEMAN

Limericks

There was a young lady of Exeter,
So pretty, that men craned their necks at her.
   One was even so brave
   As to take out and wave
The distinguishing mark of his sex at her.

1927

There's an unbroken babe from Toronto,
Exceedingly hard to get onto,
   But when you get there,
   And have parted the hair,
You can fuck her as much as you want to.

1941

A remarkable race are the Persians,
They have such peculiar diversions.
   They screw the whole day
   In the regular way,
And save up the nights for perversions.

1941

There once was a lady from Arden
Who sucked off a man in a garden.
　　He said, "My dear Flo,
　　Where does all that stuff go?"
And she said, "(swallow hard)—I beg pardon?"

1932

Then up spake the Bey of Algiers
And said to his harem, "My dears,
　　You may think it odd o' me
　　But I've given up sodomy—
Tonight there'll be fucking!" (Loud cheers.)

1910

A habit obscene and bizarre
Has taken a-hold of papa:
　　He brings home young camels
　　And other odd mammals,
And gives them a go at mama.

1946

One morning Mahatma Gandhi
Had a hard-on, and it was a dandy.
  So he said to his aide,
  "Please bring me a maid,
Or a goat, or whatever is handy."

                       1941

There was a young man from New Haven
Who had an affair with a raven.
  He said with a grin
  As he wiped off his chin,
"Nevermore!"

                       1943

There was a young lady from Cue
Who filled her vagina with glue.
  She said with a grin,
  "If they pay to get in,
They'll pay to get out of it too."

                       1947

There was a young woman of Chester
Who said to the man who undressed her,
   "I think you will find
   That it's better behind—
The front is beginning to fester."

1927

Nymphomaniacal Alice
Used a dynamite stick for a phallus.
   They found her vagina
   In North Carolina,
And her ass-hole in Buckingham Palace.

1942

A squeamish young fellow named Brand
Thought caressing his penis was grand,
   But he viewed with distaste
   The gelatinous paste
That it left in the palm of his hand.

1942

A psychoneurotic fanatic
Said, "I take little girls to the attic,
   Then whistle a tune
   'Bout the cow and the moon—
When the cow jumps I come. It's dramatic."

1946

The team of Tom and Louise
Do an act in the nude on their knees.
   They crawl down the aisle
   While fucking dog-style
And the orchestra plays Kilmer's "Trees."

1945

There was a young girl of Peru
Who had nothing whatever to do,
   So she sat on the stairs
   And counted cunt hairs—
Four thousand, three hundred, and two.

1941

There was a young man from Racine
Who invented a fucking machine.
   Concave or convex
   It would fit either sex,
With attachments for those in between.

1927

The Reverend Henry Ward Beecher
Called a girl a most elegant creature.
   So she laid on her back,
   And, exposing her crack,
Said, "Fuck that, you old Sunday School Teacher!"

1948

There was an old man from Bubungi
Whose balls were all covered with fungi.
   With his friends, out at lunch,
   He tore off a bunch
And said, "Now divide this among ye."

1941

There was a young girl from Decatur
Who was fucked by an old alligator.
  No one ever knew
  How she relished that screw,
For after he fucked her, he ate her.

1944

A disgusting young man named McGill
Made his neighbors exceedingly ill
  When they learned of his habits
  Involving white rabbits
And a bird with a flexible bill.

1944

There was a young lady of Norway
Who hung by her heels in a doorway.
  She said to her beau,
  "Look at me, Joe,
I think I've discovered one more way."

1952

From Racine: Phèdre
Act II/Scene ii

Hippolyte: Madam, could I hate you?
  No matter what they say or how they paint my pride,
  do they suppose some beast once carried me inside?
  What mind that is unkind, what heart that may be hard,
  in viewing you, would not grow soft in its regard?
  Could any man resist the charm of what you are?

Aricie: What? My Lord.

Hippolyte: But I know, now I have gone too far.
  Reason, I see, gives way to feelings that are real.
  I have already said more than I should reveal,
  Madam, so I go on: I must inform you of
  something which my own heart keeps secret in its love.
  You see before you here a wretched restless Prince,
  epitome of pride too headstrong to convince.
  I who fought love and thought my attitude was right;
  who laughed at its captives and ridiculed their plight;
  who scorned the worst shipwrecks, the first one to deplore
  the storms of mortals which I witnessed from the shore;
  now I have been bowed down to know the common lot,
  how I have been estranged and changed to what I'm not!
  One instant has destroyed my childish arrogance:
  this soul which was so bold now yields to circumstance.
  For almost six long months, so hopeless and alone,
  and bearing everywhere this torture I have known;
  divided in desires, I don't know what to do:
  with you, I try to fly; alone, I long for you;
  far off in the forest, your image follows me;
  the brilliance of the day, the night's obscurity,
  all show me the sly charm which my high pride ignores;
  all render Hippolyte a prisoner of yours.
  Now through this mad pursuit, I've lost my self-control,
  so I no longer know the scope of my own soul.
  I've lost my javelins, my chariot, my bow;
  I've lost Neptune's lessons which I learned long ago;
  the woods no longer hear loud shouts as I rejoice,
  and my horses ignore the sound of my own voice.
  perhaps the telling of a love so wild and free

might make you blush to see what you have done to me.
What foolish things to say from such a captive heart!
And what a sick victim of all your lovely art!
But you should see in me that which is very dear.
Imagine that I speak another language here;
do not reject my love for its vague awkward vow,
for I have never tried to say this until now.

(tr. William Packard)

From Paul Verlaine:
Femmes/Hombres

BALANIDE I

It is a tiny heart
with its tip in the air;
so throbbing and so fair,
the tenderest sweetheart.

Its acid bath is bright
and fiercer than the fire;
its thick drops of desire
white as lilies are white.

It's violet in hue,
and here we see it live—
the pleasure it can give
as soon as it wants to!

Like a priest at high mass,
it's full of unction now,
his blessings make us bow
as they benignly pass.

He only serves from night
to the first rays of morn,
his sacred ring is worn
black gold and it shines bright.

Then when the mass is said,
discharged the way it should,
he puts back on its hood
and wears it on his head.

(tr. William Packard)

BALANIDE II

Cock, ruddy red-headed thing,
such strong longing,
sweet penis, stiff gift of love,
ready to ram whatever
and forever
hovers below or above.

You huge ding dong of delight
which springs upright,
tumescent bird flying south
and dying to screw, screw
something as you
muscle into some dumb mouth.

As if you were a wet nurse
while my lips purse,
sucking and sucking away,
cock, my great big candy stick
which I lick and lick and lick—
no, I'm not ashamed to say,

cock, you buoy up so true,
the touch of you
is like hot satin or silk,
in my hand your glory blooms
like savage plumes
of sudden opal and milk.

Sometimes when I'm all alone
and on my own
I take you out like right now—
but watch out, my cock is mad,
I'm being bad—
so let his cock show you how!

Yes his cock is just as rare
as I prepare
to mount the mouth or the rear,
ready now to ride the steed,
driving indeed
unvanquished with all my gear.

So cock you explode and spill
your liquid fill,

then relax back to limp skin,
unused udder, a pale cloud
no longer proud—
but still ready to begin!

(tr. William Packard)

GIRLS I

You straightforward girl of the street,
how much more gladly do I greet

you than those fashionable hags
who shove me with their shopping bags

and show off all their latest clothes,
their heads are filled with nylon hose,

bitching and pushing through rich stores,
these are the true Parisian whores!

But you are a true friend to me
with all your nighttime mystery,

and even when we hit the sack
you keep a strong and boyish back.

You are a lover without fuss,
happy with just the two of us,

It takes so little of your art
to make me be a stiff upstart!

Yes, you have all the joking ways
of some young boy who can amaze

me in new kinds of sin (although
sin done in secrecy is no

sin)—your cheeks are a neat small size,
your arms are round, you have wide thighs,

and that makes up for what you may
not have in a more charming way.

You are a chum, a noble soul,
your passion is so warm, so whole,

and if you ever tried to get
new ways of putting men in debt,

you could work overtime on cock
and put your whole wardrobe in hock!

Like us, you have your sorrows too,
and tears that we would shed with you,

and if our tears were mingled thus,
there is another charm for us!

For in that pity which we share
we have a common friendship there.

You brother woman of my life,
and for this one brief night, my wife . . .

Let's go to bed, and we won't stir,
but like a cat, we'll purr and purr.

Come on, come close, let me recline
my stomach so it meets your spine,

my knees lock with your knees, my feet
with your feet underneath the sheet.

Slide your ass from your loose gown,
and let my hand slip right on down

to that warmth between your legs. Now!
We are safe to hide here somehow.

This is no peace, though so it seems.
Are you asleep? Don't have bad dreams.

I'll doze too, you straightforward girl,
my nose lost in curl after curl.

(tr. *William Packard*)

THE LITTLE HOUSE

The little house in which is his bed is the prettiest in all the
    world.
  It is made with the branches of trees, four walls of dried earth,
  and a roof of thatch.

I love it, for, since the nights have grown cold, we have slept
    there
  together: and the cooler the nights are the longer are they also.
  When I rise with the coming of the day, even I find myself
  weary.

The mattress is upon the ground: two coverlets of black wool
    cover
  our bodies, which warm each other. His body presses against
    my
  breasts. My heart throbs.

He presses me so closely that he will crush me, poor little girl
    that I
  am. But when he is within me, I know nothing more in the
  world, and they might cut off my limbs without recalling me
  from my ecstasy.

PIERRE LOUŸS

GIVE ALL TO LOVE

Give all to love;
Obey thy heart;
Friends, kindred, days,
Estate, good fame,
Plans, credit, and the Muse —
Nothing refuse.

'Tis a brave master;
Let it have scope:
Follow it utterly,
Hope beyond hope:
High and more high

It dives into noon,
With wing unspent,
Untold intent;
But it is a god,
Knows its own path,
And the outlets of the sky.

It was never for the mean;
It requireth courage stout,
Souls above doubt,
Valour unbending:
Such 'twill reward;—
They shall return
More than they were,
And ever ascending.
Leave all for love;
Yet, hear me, yet,
One word more thy heart behoved,
One pulse more of firm endeavour—
Keep thee to-day,
To-morrow, for ever,
Free as an Arab
Of thy beloved.

Cling with life to the maid;
But when the surprise,
First vague shadow of surmise,
Flits across her bosom young,
Of a joy apart from thee,
Free be she, fancy-free;

Nor thou detain her vesture's hem,
Nor the palest rose she flung
From her summer diadem.

Though thou loved her as thy self,
As a self of purer clay;
Though her parting dims the day,
Stealing grace from all alive;
Heartily know,
When half-gods go
The gods arrive.

RALPH WALDO EMERSON

From Walt Whitman

FROM I SING THE BODY ELECTRIC

1

I sing the body electric,
The armies of those I love engirth me and I engirth them,
They will not let me off till I go with them, respond to them,
And discorrupt them, and charge them full with the charge of the
    soul.

Was it doubted that those who corrupt their own bodies conceal
    themselves?
And if those who defile the living are as bad as they who defile
    the dead?
And if the body does not do fully as much as the soul?
And if the body were not the soul, what is the soul?

4

I have perceiv'd that to be with those I like is enough,
To stop in company with the rest at evening is enough,
To be surrounded by beautiful, curious, breathing, laughing flesh
    is enough,
To pass among them or touch any one, or rest my arm ever so
    lightly round his or her neck for a moment, what is this then?
I do not ask any more delight, I swim in it as in a sea.

There is something in staying close to men and women and
      looking
    on them, and in the contact and odor of them, that pleases
    the soul well,
All things please the soul, but these please the soul well.

FROM SONG OF MYSELF

11

Twenty-eight young men bathe by the shore,
Twenty-eight young men and all so friendly;
Twenty-eight years of womanly life and all so lonesome.

She owns the fine house by the rise of the bank,
She hides handsome and richly drest aft the blinds of the window.

Which of the young men does she like the best?
Ah the homeliest of them is beautiful to her.

Where are you off to, lady? for I see you,
You splash in the water there, yet stay stock still in your room.

Dancing and laughing along the beach came the twenty-ninth
    bather,
The rest did not see her, but she saw them and loved them.

The beards of the young men glisten'd with wet, it ran from their
    long hair,
Little streams pass'd all over their bodies.

An unseen hand also pass'd over their bodies,
It descended tremblingly from their temples and ribs.

The young men float on their backs, their white bellies bulge to
    the sun, they do not ask who seizes fast to them,
They do not know who puffs and declines with pendant and
    bending arch,
They do not think whom they souse with spray.

CHILDREN OF ADAM: *FROM* PENT-UP ACHING RIVERS

From pent-up aching rivers,
From that of myself without which I were nothing,
From what I am determin'd to make illustrious, even if I stand
    sole among men,
From my own voice resonant, singing the phallus,
Singing the song of procreation,
Singing the need of superb children and therein superb grown
    people,
Singing the muscular urge and the blending,
Singing the bedfellow's song, (O resistless yearning!
O for any and each the body correlative attracting!
O for you whoever you are your correlative body! O it, more than
    all else, you delighting!)
From the hungry gnaw that eats me night and day,
From native moments, from bashful pains, singing them,
Seeking something yet unfound though I have diligently sought it
    many a long year,
Singing the true song of the soul fitful at random,
Renascent with grossest Nature or among animals,
Of that, of them and what goes with them my poems informing,
Of the smell of apples and lemons, of the pairing of birds,
Of the wet of woods, of the lapping of waves,
Of the mad pushes of waves upon the land, I them chanting,
The overture lightly sounding, the strain anticipating,
The welcome nearness, the sight of the perfect body,
The swimmer swimming naked in the bath, or motionless on his
    back lying and floating,
The female form approaching, I pensive, love-flesh tremulous
    aching,
The divine list for myself or you or for any one making,
The face, the limbs, the index from head to foot, and what it
    arouses,
The mystic deliria, the madness amorous, the utter abandonment,
(Hark close and still what I now whisper to you,
I love you, O you entirely possess me,
O that you and I escape from the rest and go utterly off, free and
    lawless,

Two hawks in the air, two fishes swimming in the sea not more
    lawless than we;)
The furious storm through me careering, I passionately
      trembling,
The oath of the inseparableness of two together, of the woman
    that loves me and whom I love more than my life, that oath
    swearing,
(O I willingly stake all for you,
O let me be lost if it must be so!
O you and I! what is it to us what the rest do or think?
What is all else to us? only that we enjoy each other and exhaust
    each other if it must be so;)
From the master, the pilot I yield the vessel to,
The general commanding me, commanding all, from his permis-
    sion taking,
From time the programme hastening, (I have loiter'd too long as
     it is,)
From sex, from the warp and from the woof,
From privacy, from frequent repinings alone,
From plenty of persons near and yet the right person not near,
From the soft sliding of hands over me and thrusting of fingers
    through my hair and beard,
From the long sustain'd kiss upon the mouth or bosom,
From the close pressure that makes me or any man drunk,
     fainting with excess,
From what the divine husband knows, from the work of
    fatherhood,
From exultation, victory and relief, from the bedfellow's embrace
    in the night,
From the act-poems of eyes, hands, hips and bosoms,
From the cling of the trembling arm,
From the bending curve and the clinch,
From side by side the pliant coverlet off-throwing,
From the one so unwilling to have me leave, and me just as un-
    willing to leave,
(Yet a moment O tender waiter, and I return,)
From the hour of shining stars and dropping dews,
From the night a moment I emerging flitting out,
Celebrate you act divine and you children prepared for,
And you stalwart loins.

A WOMAN WAITS FOR ME

A woman waits for me, she contains all, nothing is lacking,
Yet all were lacking if sex were lacking, or if the moisture of the
right man were lacking.

Sex contains all, bodies, souls,
Meanings, proofs, purities, delicacies, results, promulgations,
Songs, commands, health, pride, the maternal mystery, the
seminal milk,
All hopes, benefactions, bestowals, all the passions, loves,
beauties, delights of the earth,
All the governments, judges, gods, follow'd persons of the earth,
These are contain'd in sex as parts of itself and justifications of
itself.

Without shame the man I like knows and avows the deliciousness
of his sex,
Without shame the woman I like knows and avows hers.

Now I will dismiss myself from impassive women,
I will go stay with her who waits for me, and with those women
that are warm-blooded and sufficient for me,
I see that they understand me and do not deny me,
I see that they are worthy of me, I will be the robust husband of
those women.

They are not one jot less than I am,
They are tann'd in the face by shining suns and blowing winds,
Their flesh has the old divine suppleness and strength,
They know how to swim, row, ride, wrestle, shoot, run, strike,
retreat, advance, resist, defend themselves,
They are ultimate in their own right—they are calm, clear, well-
possess'd of themselves.

I draw you close to me, you women,
I cannot let you go, I would do you good,
I am for you, and you are for me, not only for our own sake, but
for others' sakes,
Envelop'd in you sleep greater heroes and bards,
They refuse to awake at the touch of any man but me.

It is I, you women, I make my way,
I am stern, acrid, large, undissuadable, but I love you,
I do not hurt you any more than is necessary for you,
I pour the stuff to start sons and daughters fit for these States, I
    press with slow rude muscle,
I brace myself effectually, I listen to no entreaties,
I dare not withdraw till I deposit what has so long accumulated
    within me.

Through you I drain the pent-up rivers of myself,
In you I wrap a thousand onward years,
On you I graft the grafts of the best-beloved of me and America,
The drops I distil upon you shall grow fierce and athletic girls,
    new artists, musicians, and singers,
The babes I beget upon you are to beget babes in their turn,
I shall demand perfect men and women out of my love-spendings,
I shall expect them to interpenetrate with others, as I and you
    interpenetrate now,
I shall count on the fruits of the gushing showers of them, as I
    count on the fruits of the gushing showers I give now,
I shall look for loving crops from the birth, life, death,
        immortality,
    I plant so lovingly now.

THE BETROTHAL

Oh, come, my lad, or go my lad,
  And love me if you like!
I hardly hear the door shut
  Or the knocker strike.

Oh, bring me gifts or beg me gifts,
  And wed me if you will!
I'd make a man a good wife,
  Sensible and still.

And why should I be cold, my lad,
  And why should you repine,
Because I love a dark head
  That never will be mine?

I might as well be easing you
  As lie alone in bed,
And waste the night in wanting
  A cruel dark head!

You might as well be calling yours
  What never will be his,
And one of us be happy;
  There's few enough as is.

EDNA ST. VINCENT MILLAY

NATIONAL WINTER GARDEN

Outspoken buttocks in pink beads
Invite the necessary cloudy clinch
Of bandy eyes . . . No extra mufflings here:
The world's one flagrant, sweating cinch.

And while legs waken salads in the brain
You pick your blonde out neatly through the smoke.
Always you wait for someone else though, always—
(Then rush the nearest exit through the smoke).

Always and last, before the final ring
When all the fireworks blare, begins
A tom-tom scrimmage with a somewhere violin,
Some cheapest echo of them all—begins.

And shall we call her whiter than the snow?
Sprayed first with ruby, then with emerald sheen—
Least tearful and least glad (who knows her smile?)
A caught slide shows her sandstone grey between.

Her eyes exist in swivellings of her teats,
Pearls whip her hips, a drench of whirling strands.
Her silly snake rings begin to mount, surmount
Each other—turquoise fakes on tinselled hands.

We wait that writhing pool, her pearls collapsed,
—All but her belly buried in the floor;
And the lewd trounce of a final muted beat!
We feel her spasm through a fleshless door . . . .

Yet, to the empty trapeze of your flesh,
O Magdalene, each comes back to die alone.
Then you, the burlesque of our lust—and faith,
Lug us back lifeward—bone by infant bone.

HART CRANE

I KNEW A WOMAN

I knew a woman, lovely in her bones,
When small birds sighed, she would sigh back at them;
Ah, when she moved, she moved more ways than one:
The shapes a bright container can contain!
Of her choice virtues only gods should speak.
Or English poets who grew up on Greek
(I'd have them sing in chorus, cheek to cheek).

How well her wishes went! She stroked my chin,
She taught me Turn, and Counter-turn, and Stand;
She taught me Touch, that undulant white skin;
I nibbled meekly from her proffered hand;
She was the sickle; I, poor I, the rake,
Coming behind her for her pretty sake
(But what prodigious mowing we did make).

Love likes a gander, and adores a goose:
Her full lips pursed, the errant note to seize;
She played it quick, she played it light and loose;
My eyes, they dazzled at her flowing knees;
Her several parts could keep a pure repose,
Or one hip quiver with a mobile nose
(She moved in circles, and those circles moved).

Let seed be grass, and grass turn into hay:
I'm martyr to a motion not my own;
What's freedom for? To know eternity.
I swear she cast a shadow white as stone.
But who would count eternity in days?
These old bones live to learn her wanton ways:
(I measure time by how a body sways).

THEODORE ROETHKE

From Kenneth Patchen

FOR MIRIAM

The sea is awash with roses O they blow
Upon the land

The still hills fill with their scent
O the hills flow on their sweetness
As on God's hand

O love, it is so little we know of pleasure
Pleasure that lasts as the snow

But the sea is awash with roses O they blow
Upon the land

Do I not deal with angels
When her lips I touch

So gentle, so *warm and sweet*—falsity
Has no sight of her
O the world is a place of veils and roses
When she is there

I am come to her wonder
Like a boy finding a star in a haymow
And there is nothing cruel or mad or evil
Anywhere

WE TALKED OF THINGS

We talked of things but all the time we wanted each other
and finally we were silent and I knelt above your body

a closing of eyes
and falling unfalteringly
over a warm pure country and something crying

when I was a child things being hurt made me sorry
for them but it seemed the way men and women did
and we had not made the world

coming into it crying
(I wanted so not to hurt you)
and going out of it like a sudden pouring of salt

later, being tired and overflowing with tenderness
girl's body to boy's body lying there and wondering what it had
     been
we got to our feet very quietly so that they would not waken
but we felt their shy sorrowful look on us as we left them alone
     there

                    * * * * *

All things are one thing to the earth
rayless as a blind leper Blake lies with everyman
and the fat lord sleeps beside his bastard at last
and it doesn't matter, it doesn't mean what we think it does
for we two will never lie there
we shall not be there when death reaches out his sparkling hands

there are so many little dyings that it doesn't matter which of
     them is death.

23RD STREET RUNS INTO HEAVEN

You stand near the window as lights wink
On along the street. Somewhere a trolley, taking
Shop-girls and clerks home, clatters through
This before-supper Sabbath. An alley cat cries
To find the garbage cans sealed; newsboys
Begin their murder-into-pennies round.
We are shut in, secure for a little, safe until
Tomorrow. You slip your dress off, roll down
Your stockings, careful against runs. Naked now,
With soft light on soft flesh, you pause
For a moment; turn and face me—
Smile in a way that only women know
Who have lain long with their lover
And are made more virginal.

Our supper is plain but we are very wonderful.

THE WILD, PAINFUL, SPLASHING NEED
FROM THE JOURNAL OF ALBION
MOONLIGHT

The wild, painful, splashing need of a woman runs through me.
I want to crack a rock with my head and find inside it that
turning, wet, slippery-soft honey—to press hard, savagely
into it; I would tear up a tree and throw my body around it,
grinding, twisting, shoving—feeling a woman's flesh drowning
under me, the sweet, blubbery spit on her lips, the smell of
her hair, Jesus! the whole dizzy pure vile ravaged wonder of
my hands cutting into her thighs and the little gulping puppy-
        sounds
she makes . . . the incense of that sharp, half-bitter womansweat
as she worships what we are doing . . .

DIONYSUS

When Eubolus the Greek learned
that his wife had taken
    a lover
he cried a little
   with the smart of it
and then
    to her marvelling delight—
his appetite increased by vanity—
   tupped her eight times
   before the sun roused up:
a phallus hung in the whitening sky
bringing peace to their humid limbs.

IRVING LAYTON

CELEBRATION

When you kneel below me
and in both your hands
hold my manhood like a sceptre,

When you wrap your tongue
about the amber jewel
and urge my blessing,

I understand those Roman girls
who danced around a shaft of stone
and kissed it till the stone was warm.

Kneel, love, a thousand feet below me,
so far I can barely see your mouth and hands
perform the ceremony,

Kneel till I topple to your back
with a groan, like those gods on the roof
that Samson pulled down.

LEONARD COHEN

THE CONFESSOR

Father . . . —Say the confiteor. —I said it.—
The act of contrition? —I already done it.—
Continue, then. —I said crazy prick
To my husband, and I lifted four bits.—

Then? —For a pot my cat broke on me
I said before I knew it: "Goddam you!"
I know, it's a critter of God! —What else? —Well,
I went to bed with a young man that I know.—

And what happened there? —A bit of everything.—
That is? The usual way, I should imagine.—
And from the rear . . . —Oh, what a ghastly sin!

Therefore, because of this young man, return,
My daughter, with a heart fully contrite,
Tomorrow, at my own house, around midnight.

G.G. Belli
(tr. Harold Norse)

THE BALLAD OF THE LONELY
MASTURBATOR

The end of the affair is always death.
She's my workshop. Slippery eye,
out of the tribe of myself my breath
finds you gone. I horrify
those who stand by. I am fed.
At night, alone, I marry the bed.

Finger to finger, now she's mine.
She's not too far. She's my encounter.
I beat her like a bell. I recline
in the bower where you used to mount her.
You borrowed me on the flowered spread.
At night, alone, I marry the bed.

Take for instance this night, my love,
that every single couple puts together
with a joint overturning, beneath, above,
the abundant two on sponge and feather,
kneeling and pushing, head to head.
At night, alone, I marry the bed.

I break out of my body this way,
an annoying miracle. Could I
put the dream market on display?
I am spread out. I crucify.
My little plum is what you said.
At night, alone, I marry the bed.

Then my black-eyed rival came.
The lady of water, rising on the beach,
a piano at her fingertips, shame
on her lips and a flute's speech.
And I was the knock-kneed broom instead.
At night, alone, I marry the bed.

She took you the way a woman takes
a bargain dress off the rack
and I broke the way a stone breaks.
I give back your books and fishing tack.
Today's paper says that you are wed.
At night, alone, I marry the bed.

The boys and girls are one tonight.
They unbutton blouses. They unzip flies.
They take off shoes. They turn off the light.
The glimmering creatures are full of lies.
They are eating each other. They are overfed.
At night, alone, I marry the bed.

ANNE SEXTON

CUNTS

(Upon Receiving the Swingers Life Club Membership Solicitation)

Venus de Milo didn't have one, at least no pussy
that left its shadow in the marble, but Botticelli's Venus,
though we cannot see it for her sea-anemone hand,
did, no doubt—an amber-furred dear mouth we would kiss
could we enter the Arcadian plane of the painting.
We must assimilate cunts to our creed of beauty.
September Morn held her thighs tight shut, and the dolls
we grew up undressing had nothing much there, not even MADE
    IN USA,
but the beauties we must learn to worship now all
have spread legs, splayed in bedspreaded motel beds,
and the snowflakes that burst forth are no two alike:
sweet T-bones of hair, lips lurid as strips of salmon,
whirlpooly wisps more ticklish than skin, black brooms
a witch could ride cackling through the cold stars,
and assholes a-stare like monocles tiny as dimes.

"I adore french culture and can really blow your mind"
"half of an ultra-sophisticated couple who prefers"
"love modelling with guys or gals and groovy parties"
"affectionate young housewife would like to meet"
"attractive broadminded funloving exotic tastes'"
glory Gloria fellatio Felicia Connie your cunt
is Platonism upside down and really opens innocence
the last inch wider: I bite and I believe.

Who put this mouse between my legs if not the Lord?
Who knocks to enter? Pigs of many stripes.
My cunt is me, it lathers and it loves
because its emptiness knows nothing else to do.
Here comes the stalwart cock, numb-headed hater,
assassin dragging behind him in a wrinkled sack
reproduction's two stooges; refrigerated in blood,
the salt sperm thrashes to mix with my lipstick.
Nibble my nipples, you fish. My eyelashes tickle your glans
while my cunt like a shark gone senile yawns for its meal.
In my prison your head will lean against the wet red wall
and beg for a pardon and my blood will beat back No.

THIS IS HOW I LIKE IT

This is how I like it.
On my back, with Karen
over me. Would you like
to hear the details,
Mama? Maybe I could show
you, some night when you
have guests for dinner.
I could lie down on the
living room floor and show
how we use our fingers,
how I twist and turn.
It would be like having
a daughter that played
the piano. You didn't
know anything about this
before, I know, because
this is the first time
my diary's been home
all year. But I know
too you'll find out now,
when you look in my
drawers to see what I'm
hiding. So here it is, Mama,
enjoy it. And when Karen
comes home with me this
summer you can watch us
together, if you believe
me, watch how our hands
almost touch, watch
how we laugh when
we look at you.

LOLA HASKINS

Here is my being, my jewel, simpler than a diamond,
finer-spun than Assyrian gold and the Book of Kells,
nobler than a theorem by Euler, more darling than a dimple
in a Steuben-glass Shirley Temple, flesh-flower, riddle
of more levels than a Pyramid passageway greased with balm.
Adore!"

A woman once upon a bed with me
to kiss my heart went down but in addition thrust
her ass up to my face and trembled all her length
so I knew something rare was being served; of course
the lapping was an ecstasy, but such as ecstasy
I prayed her distant face grow still so I could drink
the deeper of this widening self that only lacked
the prick of stars to be a firmament.

Adore
this hole that bleeds with the moon so we can be born.
Stretched like a howl between the feet pushing the stirrups
the poor slit yields the bubble of a skull.
Glad tunnel of life, foretaste of resurrection,
slick applicant of appropriate friction
springing loose the critical honey from the delirious bee.

"You can meet these swinging gals" "you
can be in direct contact with these free-thinking modern people"
"if you are a polaroid photography enthusiast"
"you can rest assured your membership"
"you will discover the most exquisite, intimate"
"you"   and the clitoris
like a little hurt girl turns its face to the corner.

Well, how were we to know that all you fat sweethearts
were as much the vagina's victims as the poor satyr who sells
his great-aunt's IBM preferred to procure three whores
to have three ways at once—by land, by sea, by air?
"It was all a sacred mush of little pips to me."
Now you tell us, tell us and tell us, of a doorbell
crocheted of swollen nerves beneath the fur
and all the pallid moon from scalp to toes decuple
not quite this molehill of a mountain is
the Mare of Disenchantment, the Plain of No Response.
Who could have known, when you are edible all over?
So edible we gobble even your political views
as they untwist in lamplight, like lemon peel from a knife.

"And it is true, something vital ebbs from the process
once the female is considered not a monstrous emissary
from the natural darkness but as possessing, also
and simply, personhood" (a lone tear clouds
its single eye, an angel choked on ichor)
"and nevertheless" (no shadows live on marble
like these that coat my helpless hands)
"even in this flaccid later age" (the split
banana second when) "some semen
in good faith leaps" and your (unmentionable)
enhouses the comic stranger with a pinch
"I'm available . . . and so are hundreds of other
eager young girls who are ready to pose FOR YOU!"
Corinna, even your shit has something to be said for it
"avante garde of a new era of freedom" (Coronet)
"dawn of a cultural phenomenon" (Playboy)
"Dr. Gilbert Bartell, the renowned cultural anthropologist"
"page after page of totally rewarding sexual knowledge
that will be an invaluable asset in your search for greater
sexual understanding Only through complete understanding
can man hope" "Discretion is our middle name!"
Daphne, your fortune moistens. Stand. Bend down. Smile.

JOHN UPDIKE

Lip was a man wl
He used it when
With his friend's
With either sex a

BA

in this modern age of
relationships
we are all very clever.

in case you don't wor
I have 4 back ups.

4. well, that's good,

how many you got?

well, now—

one and
two and, ah, there's,
and the one in Berke
and there's yes, there
5. 5, that's
it.

she blinks.

there will never be a
male and female so
exists upon earth or
elsewhere.

Here is my being, my jewel, simpler than a diamond,
finer-spun than Assyrian gold and the Book of Kells,
nobler than a theorem by Euler, more darling than a dimple
in a Steuben-glass Shirley Temple, flesh-flower, riddle
of more levels than a Pyramid passageway greased with balm.
Adore!"

    A woman once upon a bed with me
to kiss my heart went down but in addition thrust
her ass up to my face and trembled all her length
so I knew something rare was being served; of course
the lapping was an ecstasy, but such as ecstasy
I prayed her distant face grow still so I could drink
the deeper of this widening self that only lacked
the prick of stars to be a firmament.

       Adore
this hole that bleeds with the moon so we can be born.
Stretched like a howl between the feet pushing the stirrups
the poor slit yields the bubble of a skull.
Glad tunnel of life, foretaste of resurrection,
slick applicant of appropriate friction
springing loose the critical honey from the delirious bee.

"You can meet these swinging gals" "you
can be in direct contact with these free-thinking modern people"
"if you are a polaroid photography enthusiast"
"you can rest assured your membership"
"you will discover the most exquisite, intimate"
"you"   and the clitoris
like a little hurt girl turns its face to the corner.

Well, how were we to know that all you fat sweethearts
were as much the vagina's victims as the poor satyr who sells
his great-aunt's IBM preferred to procure three whores
to have three ways at once—by land, by sea, by air?
"It was all a sacred mush of little pips to me."
Now you tell us, tell us and tell us, of a doorbell
crocheted of swollen nerves beneath the fur
and all the pallid moon from scalp to toes decuple
not quite this molehill of a mountain is
the Mare of Disenchantment, the Plain of No Response.
Who could have known, when you are edible all over?
So edible we gobble even your political views
as they untwist in lamplight, like lemon peel from a knife.

"And it is true, something vital ebbs from the process
once the female is considered not a monstrous emissary
from the natural darkness but as possessing, also
and simply, personhood" (a lone tear clouds
its single eye, an angel choked on ichor)
"and nevertheless" (no shadows live on marble
like these that coat my helpless hands)
"even in this flaccid later age" (the split
banana second when) "some semen
in good faith leaps" and your (unmentionable)
enhouses the comic stranger with a pinch
"I'm available . . . and so are hundreds of other
eager young girls who are ready to pose FOR YOU!"
Corinna, even your shit has something to be said for it
"avante garde of a new era of freedom" (Coronet)
"dawn of a cultural phenomenon" (Playboy)
"Dr. Gilbert Bartell, the renowned cultural anthropologist"
"page after page of totally rewarding sexual knowledge
that will be an invaluable asset in your search for greater
sexual understanding Only through complete understanding
can man hope" "Discretion is our middle name!"
Daphne, your fortune moistens. Stand. Bend down. Smile.

JOHN UPDIKE

LIP

Lip was a man who used his head.
He used it when he went to bed
With his friend's wife, and with his friend,
With either sex at either end.

J.V. CUNNINGHAM

BACK UPS

in this modern age of love/sex
relationships
we are all very clever.

in case you don't work, she tells me,
I have 4 back ups.

4. well, that's good, I say.

how many you got? she asks.

well, now—

one and
two and, ah, there's, yes, 3,
and the one in Berkeley, that's 4,
and there's yes, there's
5. 5, that's
it.

she blinks.

there will never be any rest between the
male and female so long as more than one of each
exists upon earth or
elsewhere.

CHARLES BUKOWSKI

THIS IS HOW I LIKE IT

This is how I like it.
On my back, with Karen
over me. Would you like
to hear the details,
Mama? Maybe I could show
you, some night when you
have guests for dinner.
I could lie down on the
living room floor and show
how we use our fingers,
how I twist and turn.
It would be like having
a daughter that played
the piano. You didn't
know anything about this
before, I know, because
this is the first time
my diary's been home
all year. But I know
too you'll find out now,
when you look in my
drawers to see what I'm
hiding. So here it is, Mama,
enjoy it. And when Karen
comes home with me this
summer you can watch us
together, if you believe
me, watch how our hands
almost touch, watch
how we laugh when
we look at you.

LOLA HASKINS

GREEN JELLO

"Let's make love in a bathtub
full of green jello," he said

It took twenty seven packages
half a tub of hot water
half a tub of cold
a cold night to make it set

We stepped in
squishy . . . spongey
wobbling, bobbling
jello jumping

Breasts like a sagging mold
Penis like a lime popsicle
wishing we had remembered
the fruit cocktail

since it took two weeks
to return to normal color

LINDA KING

watching them very carefully
i learned the female position
seeing another male coming
i got down on all fours
arching my back downward
my stomach touched the grass
approaching me with interest
he slowly inhaled my species
walking around behind me
he sniffed my vagina with interest
mounting me from the rear
his stomach brushed my back
backward and forward
forward and backward
as the mule entered

LINDA LAHEY

COUNTERFEITERS

The dust of darkness
Fills the room.

The counterfeiters next door
Are making dollars, credit cards,
Plastic mushrooms and caviar,
Plastic cars and yachts,
Plastic days and nights.
I can hear their power presses
And photocopy equipment
Humming.
They work even in their dreams.

You and I lie in our black bed,
Wild in our poverty,
Counterfeiting love.
You tell me you worship mountains;
I tell you I worship valleys.
Is this art or a lie?

Can two pretenses add up to a truth?

STEPHEN STEPANCHEV

LOOKING AT EACH OTHER

Yes, we were looking at each other
Yes, we knew each other very well
Yes, we had made love with each other many times
Yes, we had heard music together
Yes, we had gone to the sea together
Yes, we had cooked and eaten together
Yes, we had laughed often day and night
Yes, we fought violence and knew violence
Yes, we hated the inner and outer oppression
Yes, that day we were looking at each other
Yes, we saw the sunlight pouring down
Yes, the corner of the table was between us
Yes, bread and flowers were on the table
Yes, our eyes saw each other's eyes
Yes, our mouths saw each other's mouth
Yes, our breasts saw each other's breasts
Yes, our bodies entire saw each other
Yes, it was beginning in each
Yes, it threw waves across our lives
Yes, the pulses were becoming very strong
Yes, the beating became very delicate
Yes, the calling   the arousal
Yes, the arriving   the coming
Yes, there it was for both entire
Yes, we were looking at each other

MURIEL RUKEYSER

83RD ODE FOR IRIS — 4:55 AM
THURS 16 SEPT 1970
—FIRST NEW YORK POEM AFTER VERMONT

After all the trouble we've
been thru together, now to've
had such a fuck together!
Iris! Dear

Iris!—So good to meet you!
So good to come together!
(cliché goal of the sex books . . .
I see why . . .).

I love to make you feel good!
(I say this to two others,
& mean it every time
I say it.)

But even more, to come to
a climax of feeling good
myself at the same time you
come to one!:

That's something else again, dear
love, curious love, Iris!:
What you used to want so much
has happened!

JACKSON MacLow

From Siv Cedering

WHEN I WAS GODIVA

When I was Godiva
with the long hair
ready to ride
the streets in anger,

I cut my hair short!
for even naked nipples
could not make them see
what was naked in me.

But now,
before the mirror,
I cover myself with

my hair,
grown long again,
thinking how you will

lift it,
above my shoulders,
to look at me.

POMEGRANATES

You take me to the woods
Where the sun is still warm
On brown leaves
You show me how to squeeze
    The fruit
Bite a small hole
    And suck

Fresh water sifted in soil
Drawn by roots to rise
In the trunk
To be red and sweet
    in the fruit
And yet sweeter
    in my mouth
Before I give you
    To drink

ORNITHOLOGY

The woodcock rises
in a complicated dance.
The cardinal has color.
The lark has song.
And some small birds
attract their mates
with intricate
constructions.

I brush my hair,
wear bright colors and
French perfume,
and walk around
my garden,

kick a pebble and
pick a rose,
lift the rose up
to my lips
to feel a petal:
penis skin.

IMAGINE!

It was not alright with her,
the lying together times.

She wanted me to come
to the town of her doll house
and ask her.

Self righteously I fumed.
The air blew up in my curses.
How could a woman travel with you
and ask you to come and
ask her.

LEO CONNELLAN

TWO SONGS

1

Give me a love
That has never been,
Deeper than thought.
Make the earth move,
The desert green
After long drought.

In the flesh, leaf,
In the bones, root,
The gardener's hand
Untangles grief,
Invents a land.

2

What other lover
Could ever displace
Despair with all-heal
Or help me uncover
Sweet herb of grace
In the desolate field?

None had your face —
So pure in its poise,
So closed in its power,
That disciplined place
Where the tragic joys
Flower and re-flower.

MAY SARTON

POEM

Your flowering gave you title:
the first breasts to sprout
on our long street that sloped
to games in the garden house.
We sat among pots & spades
tall rubber boots & springing
rakes & I was careful to
disguise my eyes—punish my
open face by breathing
heavily into my arms while
my brother warmed those first &
winning fruits in his two
hands as a blaze of quiet
flourished in vacant lots.

MICHAEL HARLOW

ARETHUSA SPEAKS TO ALPHEUS AS HE PURSUES HER

"Teacher of strange ways is Love, maker of mischief,
With his magical spell he taught a river to dive."

MOSCHUS, Alexandrian poet

You offer your cock as something I could
use. The shape is handsome, unmarked as a
new mushroom, I will admit. Responsive,
intelligent, you say. I could teach it
to perform, move upon command, come and
fetch me strings of lapis, azure or gold.
A tent over your shaft, my cunt could fold,
take shape, rise as moist pliable canvas
filled like a sail on the mast of a ship.
My mouth around it would say only that
like the sea, your cock lacks perfume, tastes of
salt. There must be talent to raise it high
above the ordinary. Does it sing?
Though the shape is suggestive, I can't use
it to stir my soups, or pen my poems but
I'll keep my hand in your pocket for one
week, if I must, and learn your ebb and flow.
Now it seems tame enough while I stroke it,
a tired fish, slightly damp. Good god! It moves.
Who trained it to live erect and hard in
air without wet warmth, or taught it to grow
like a prickly pear cactus? Will it bloom?
I must tell you that I have two deft hands,
plenty for my need. You might take their place.
I only ask that you never climb in
bed and grab my genitals, a blind limb
thrusting toward heat. Begin with my throat,
lips treacherous from solitude that shape
and speak empty promises to mere men.
Become a stream, make your way far under
bushes, dive deep in my tunnel, mingle
your water with mine. Let the fountain spray.

VIVIAN SHIPLEY-JOKL

BLUE CONCORDS

Like sucking dark September grapes
to lie here sucking you

slippery as Concords under your skin
a tease away in your sack

like a pouch of prize aggies—

cats' eyes—

liquid in their dark.

JEAN BALDERSTON

CORNSILK

When I rub you
the lips between my legs
grow fat as padded silk.

And the hairs of our hair
tangle and squeak
coarse and sweet as cornsilk.

Your cob gleams teeth
and milk.

JEAN BALDERSTON

LYRIC FROM GAIETY, A FARCE

Queer's Song

Floating, face up, on the open
    Estuary
Of sleep, you wait for it to happen.
    You are very

Beautiful, stupid, and alone
    Now at the source
Of all the loneliness we learn
    From someone else.

For you the darkness does its part—
    Arms fall, and eyes,
And the heart proves by its lack an art
    The mouth supplies.

Sleep then, or feign to, as you drown
    And I pursue
Your blood to its filthy cellar down
    In the hollow

Hairy places. Here shall I feed
    Where every sense,
Handmaid and Hangman to your need,
    Is audience.

RICHARD HOWARD

PROPERTY SETTLEMENT

As we bought the furniture
we thought it would root us together:
every chair would be a child,
every mirror a glass for our passion,
every painting a patch of cracked wall
covered & covered forever.

But now we are moving on—
& all our treasured junk
which seemed so solid, so unmoveable,
is like ashes in the fist of a mourner
outside the crematorium.

Scatter it over the sea!
I am moving to a bare house on a bluff
overlooking the Pacific.
I will furnish it with the multicolored love
of my red-bearded, green-eyed lover,
with the crushed kaleidoscope of our passion,
& the bottle glass we find along the beach,
& the pure unclouded sunlight that we pour
over & over each other.
If we don't have a bed,
we will make nourishing love
on the sunstruck kitchen floor.
If we don't have a chair,
we will rock
on each other's thighs.
If we don't have a table,
we will eat out of each other's
delicious bodies.
He will lick honey from my cunt,
I will cover his cock with jam
& suck it off like a hungry baby.

Take the desk, the analytic couch,
the posters we bought in dead Vienna.
Take the scholarly journals, the brokerage receipts,
the money, the money, the money,
& churn your worthless stock.
Put coins in your pocket;
they will not buy you love.
Make a blanket of bonds & passbooks;

they will not keep you warm.
Quilt yourself over with checks;
they will not bounce for you as I did.

You will be solvent & sane
huddled in the coinage of your coldness—
but I am gone.

ERICA JONG

THE PUZZLE

They locked into each other
like brother & sister,
long-lost relations,
orphans divided by time.

He bit her shoulder
& entered her blood forever.
She bit his tongue
& changed the tone of his song.

They walked together astonished
not to be lonely.
They sought their loneliness
like lost dogs.

But they were joined together
by tongue & shoulder.
His nightmares woke her;
her daydreams startled him.

He fucked so hard
he thought he'd climb back in her.
She came so hard
her skin seemed to dissolve.

She feared she had no yearning
left to write with.
He feared she'd suck him dry
& glide away.

They spoke of all these things
& locked together.
She figured out
the jigsaw of his heart.

& he unscrambled her
& placed the pieces
with such precision
nothing came apart.

ERICA JONG

TO A CLITORIS

Hot, moist obscenities of orchids
Glide delirium to smooth obsession
Like Siren-singing invidious Ids'
Enlipped insistence in lush progression,
Stickly redolence reverberating
Along soft column, around labellum
(Luscious landing for the pollinating)
Over the nectar cup—smell of welcome!
Ambrosial lure from thy nectaries
Fecundly flows and glistens, spellbinding
Tongue, that dreamslides in loose trajectories
To kiss the anther (Little Feller)—Ping!

Tonight clitoral hymns, forgetting fuck,
Call us, vibrato, to a swoon of suck.

HARRY SMITH

READING ROOM, THE NEW YORK PUBLIC LIBRARY

In the reading room in the New York Public Library
All sorts of souls were bent over silent reading the past,
Or the present, or maybe it was the future, persons
Devoted to silence and the flowering of the imagination,
When all of a sudden I saw my love,
She was a faun with light steps and brilliant eye
And she came walking among the tables and rows of persons,

Straight from the forest to the center of New York,
And nobody noticed, or raised an eyelash.
These were fixed on imaginary splendours of the past,
Or of the present, or maybe of the future, maybe
Something as seductive as the aquiline nose
Of Eleanor of Aquitaine, or Cleopatra's wrist-locket in Egypt,
Or maybe they were thinking of Juliana of Norwich.

The people of this world pay no attention to the fauns
Whether of this world or of another, but there she was,
All gaudy pelt, and sleek, gracefully moving,
Her amber eye was bright among the porticoes,
Her delicate ears were raised to hear of love,
Her lips had the appearance of green grass
About to be trodden, and her shanks were smooth and sleek.

Everybody was in the splendour of his imagination,
Nobody paid any attention to this splendour
Appearing in the New York Public Library,
Their eyes were on China, India, Arabia, or the Balearics,
While my faun was walking among the tables and eyes
Inventing their world of life, invisible and light,
In silence and sweet temper, loving the world.

RICHARD EBERHART

SEX POEM

1. prologue

right now as
i am talking
to you

are trillions
of tiny
neutrinos

are
passing
through me

and in this
next instant
they are

out there on the
other side of
our solar system

    we are all of us
    living in the middle
    of a libidinal field

are such strong
currents running
through us always

each instant
of our inner
lives

so it is no
wonder we reach
out to each other

i want you
to eat the air
of where i am right now

i want you to
feel me wading
waist high

through the field
of your wide
open thighs

i want
this instant
to blossom

endlessly
in your own
bloodstream

so that
someday
ages away

from where
we are
right now

you may be able
to look back
and remember

the way i am
talking to you
right now

2. seduction

why do i
always feel
everyone else knows

all about
sex
except me

   how do you
   do how do
   you do it

if we were
in ancient Greece
right now

we could
go see
fertility rites

as if sex
were a
sacrament

that had
to be
practiced

   how do you
   do how do
   you do it

but here is
only our own
raw dreams

and so we have
to figure out
all about

what we want
and how we want
to want it

3. undress

why don't we
take all our
clothes off

so i can
see your
spooky boobs

is they
enormous
nipples

or is they
tiny
tits

and does
they pucker up
they little tips

aw go on
take all your
clothes off

so i can see
the cute fluff
of tuft

is down there
on your outstanding
mound

come on
let's take our
clothes off

4. foreplay

we are
like a couple
of kids

who delight
in toying
with each other

let me lick
at your
clit

so it
perks up
pert and saucy

there in
your most
secret place

where there
is a moist
musk smell

and you can suck
on my ruddy
red-headed thing

so it will stick
up straight
rock hard

throbbing god
and buoyed up
on its own merits

so we
will
know

the
pulse of
possibility

in
every
body part

5. penetration

at last i
enter into
you at last

i have never
known such pure
floating

as i know right
now in your sweet
jesus vagina

    is in
    thank god
    is in

my christ we
could stay this
way forever

6. orgasm

now pounding
down hard now
pounding down

hard such
good strong
strokes

i thrust
and yield
i thrust and

yield like
some great
wood oar

that works
against the great
weight of water

    until we
    are both so
    close to closure

is like a
great wave
racing on its

way to break
against the slippery
glistening rocks

    crash and shatter
    in a catastrophe
    of satisfaction

and all those
trillions of tiny
microscopic sperm

go swimming
on up into
you

tails lashing
fast through all
that amniotic fluid

7. *aftermath*

we lie together
here wondering
what was it

was all that
pounding down we did
a few moments ago

now there is
no pounding
down

is only
our own
aura

as we go
wading in
a lake

where ducks
receive
instruction

and swans float
out alone in
their serenity

    until an electric
    crack goes right
    across our braincave

we sit up
straight and
light a cigarette

then get ready
to put on our
clothes again

to go out
into that
other world

WILLIAM PACKARD

I JUST WANT TO ASK A COUPLE OF QUESTIONS

about the mechanics of men loving other men.
I mean I want to know
the order in which things happen
and whether or not there's a lot of kissing.
I've also wondered about fidelity and laughter
and that strange line:
"Lay your sleeping head, my love."
For example, who says what first
and how does it actually begin?
Do you take off your clothes slowly
and does he hold you in front of him
for a few moments? I know
one thing inevitably leads to another
but I can't picture it completely,
or maybe there's a reason I don't want to.
Once you've gotten started can you stop?
Do the two of you sometimes pause
and remember other lovers?
I mean in the middle of everything?
Does one of you get grape juice afterwards?
Would you ever let a girl watch?
I know about kneeling, licking, etc.,
but what I'm really interested in
is the other thing, and mostly how
you actually get to that,
which seems so much more serious
and, I used to think, unbelievable.
Still, there are probably all kinds of variations
impossible for me to appreciate.
Yet even though it's never the same
I keep thinking there must be basic things
you do together and that I could get a sense
of that if it were explained right.
It's hard to see the pieces.
I mean the role, say, your hands would play.
Then I think, too, it has to hurt,
at least some of the time. But is that okay?
That could be better, I've been told,
but I didn't believe it completely.

The easiest part is the kissing,
which I can perfectly imagine since I've frequently seen it.
And I like to look long when I see it,
but then I think the lovers think I'm disapproving
if I stare. Maybe a simple comparison
would clear it up for me. A comparison
that was not the usual kind
but that took in anything that even got close to the truth.
The problem is not that I can't set the scene in my mind
but that the details sort of evaporate
and I'm left trying to comprehend
a story which begins where other stories end.

PATRICA FAREWELL

THE PERVERT

Before you love me, let me say . . .
        Don't say it.
I love you for what you are. I don't need words.

But you should know that when consumed by passion
I sometimes have an uncontrollable urge . . .

Don't say it. What seems right to you will surely
seem right to me—and, well, if not, I may
silently signal in the dark. Don't spoil it
by talking about it in the light of day.

But you were talking about it at the table
with friends who read about it in a book.

You mean . . . ?

        Yes, that's exactly what I mean.

Why did you have to say it?

        Darling, look . . .

I will not look! That sort of thing is not
the sort of thing we can talk about alone.

But when consumed by passion we may do it?

I'll scream. Such things are simply never done.

JUDSON JEROME

ELEGY FOR THE OTHER WOMAN

May the plane of the other woman explode
with just one fatality.
But should it not, may the other woman spew
persistent dysentery from
your first night ever after.
May the other woman vomit
African bees and Argentine wasps.
May cobras uncoil from her loins.
May she be eaten not by something dramatic
like lions, but merely by
a particularly homely wart-hog.
I do not wish the other woman
to fall down a well
for fear of spoiling the water,
nor die on the highway because
she might obstruct traffic.
Rather: something easy and cheap,
like clap contracted en route
from some other bloke.
And should she nevertheless still survive
all these critical possibilities,
may she quietly die of boredom with you.

ELISAVIETTA RITCHIE

UP FROM FONDLE

Starting at a point
  of acting fond
and going quite
  beyond
she saw him wave
  the magic wand
then went too far
  for only fond!

KEN MCLAREN

FROM LOLITA

Frigid gentlewomen of the jury! I had thought that months, perhaps years, would elapse before I dared to reveal myself to Dolores Haze; but by six she was wide awake, and by six fifteen we were technically lovers. I am going to tell you something very strange: it was she who seduced me.

Upon hearing her first morning yawn, I feigned handsome profiled sleep. I just did not know what to do. Would she be shocked at finding me by her side, and not in some spare bed? Would she collect her clothes and lock herself up in the bathroom? Would she demand to be taken at once to Ramsdale—to her mother's bedside—back to camp? But my Lo was a sportive lassie. I felt her eyes on me, and when she uttered at last that beloved chortling note of hers, I knew her eyes had been laughing. She rolled over to my side, and her warm brown hair came against my collarbone. I gave a mediocre imitation of waking up. We lay quietly. I gently caressed her hair, and we gently kissed. Her kiss, to my delirious embarrassment, had some rather comical refinements of flutter and probe which made me conclude she had been coached at an early age by a little Lesbian. No Charlie boy could have taught her *that*. As if to see whether I had my fill and learned the lesson, she drew away and surveyed me. Her cheekbones were flushed, her full underlip glistened, my dissolution was near. All at once, with a burst of rough glee (the sign of the nymphet!), she put her mouth to my ear—but for quite a while my mind could not separate into words the hot thunder of her whisper, and she laughed, and brushed the hair off her face, and tried again, and gradually the odd sense of living in a brand new, mad new dream world, where everything was permissible, came over me as I realized what she was suggesting. I answered I did not know what game she and Charlie had played. "You mean you have never—?"—her features twisted into a stare of disgusted incredulity. "You have never—" she started again. I took time out by nuzzling her a little. "Lay off, will you," she said with a twangy whine, hastily removing her brown shoulder from my lips. (It was very curious the way she considered—and kept doing so for a long time—all caresses except kisses on the mouth or the stark act of love either "romantic slosh" or "abnormal".)

"You mean," she persisted, now kneeling above me, "you never did it when you were a kid?"

"Never," I answered quite truthfully.

"Okay," said Lolita, "here is where we start."

However, I shall not bore my learned readers with a detailed account of Lolita's presumption. Suffice it to say that not a trace of modesty did I perceive in this beautiful hardly formed young girl whom modern co-education, juvenile mores, the campfire racket and so forth had utterly and hopelessly depraved. She saw the stark act merely as part of a youngster's furtive world, unknown to adults. What adults did for purposes of procreation was no business of hers. My life was handled by little Lo in an energetic, matter-of-fact manner as if it were an insensate gadget unconnected with me. While eager to impress me with the world of tough kids, she was not quite prepared for certain discrepancies between a kid's life and mine. Pride alone prevented her from giving up; for, in my strange predicament, I feigned supreme stupidity and had her have her way—at least while I could still bear it. But really these are irrelevant matters; I am not concerned with so-called "sex" at all. Anybody can imagine those elements of animality. A greater endeavor lures me on: to fix once for all the perilous magic of nymphets.

VLADIMIR NABOKOV

FROM PASSION PLAY

They rose. Fabian led Vanessa, who was carrying her clothes, toward the sauna. Opening the door before her, he switched on the light. A smell of shavings and dry bark spilled over them; the benches, bleached and plain, offered spare comfort.

Vanessa went toward the benches, her towel abandoned, and deliberately put her clothes on the top bench. Then she sat on the one beneath waiting for him.

He began to undress, placing each item of his clothing beside the small mound Vanessa had made on the top bench. To find the freedom that had been his with her before, he willed himself to remember images of afternoons in his VanHome, of Vanessa undressing before him, carefully placing her clothes within reach in case they might be interrupted and she would have to dress quickly. He realized that then, in the conspiracy of his VanHome, it had been he who took her, a mere girl, for his lover, putting at stake the only security he knew, containing his need for her, restraining the impulse to break the seal that bound her to herself. Now it was she who was taking him for her lover, bidding him to come, inviting him to break that seal.

Naked, his body was not yet responsive. He sat down next to her, his shoulder lingering at her back, the scent of her hair mingling with the pungent smell of wood, his mouth on her neck, his lips grazing the soft mound behind her ear, soft as it had been when he had first kissed it. His hands slid over her breasts, and the stir that rose in her quickened him, but his knees did not urge her to part her legs. A disquiet that he might soon cause her pain grew in him. He wondered whether she was also apprehensive.

He slipped a hand between her thighs, skimming her flesh, brushing its folds; his fingers, deeper still, found her moist. Slowly, unresisted, his hand invaded; a force within her, he drew her to his side, her eyes on him, her arms swaddling him. Memory and thought drowned in a touch he could no longer flee, as if the knowledge of who he was lay within her, and only by claiming her could he discover it.

He bent her gently to the wooden plank, her head back, her legs spread, one angled to rest a foot on the floor, one snaring his hip as he lowered himself, his hand braced to ease his weight on her, the other hand guiding the crest of his flesh along her crease, still reluctant to sink into flesh that had abandoned resistance, the tautness in his groin rising. She arched both legs girdling his hips, and impaled herself on him, and he yielded, his flesh sinking into her, wedging her flesh until it found its obstacle, a limit of tension which seemed at one with his own urgency. He sensed the straining of her neck; her eyes, hooded, defied his scrutiny. He bore down, her nails knifing his skin, until he pierced her, breaking through to the spasm of her brief, harsh cry, the signal that he was free now to enter her deeper, to gather himself in her, swift in his motion, to reach her where she had never been reached before. Her face was distorted in a grimace, at once that of a young girl on the brink of tears and that of a woman in labor. Her hand commanding his hips, she began to thrust at Fabian, her body springing back as the tip of his flesh met her womb.

Above the sound of their breathing, Fabian heard the rasping of her teeth, a wailing from her closed mouth, its lower lip tightly bound against the other, as if to cover the scar. His hands were under her buttocks, lifting her, his flesh breaching her still further, each stroke a summons to her womb. Pushing her shoulders sideways, she curved her belly to him, her hands above her head, fingers clawing the wood as if to scrawl on it, her body sundered, waiting for him to keel into her, offering herself to a deeper quest.

He felt a warm trickle on his thigh, and he knew it to be her blood. Yet he did not lift his eyes from her face. Fusion with a body that had become his, a port of incessant entry and departure, left him uncertain whether with each step he was binding her closer to himself or setting her adrift, to shores and reaches of her own.

JERZY KOSINSKI